Top Ten Reasons to Leave the EU

John Petley

www.BretwaldaBooks.com
@Bretwaldabooks
bretwaldabooks.blogspot.co.uk/
Bretwalda Books on Facebook

First Published 2014

Bretwalda Books
Unit 8, Fir Tree Close, Epsom,
Surrey KT17 3LD
info@BretwaldaBooks.com
www.BretwaldaBooks.com
ISBN 978-1-909698-94-9

CONTENTS

Introduction

A few months ago, hardly anyone had heard of him. His country's main claim to fame was scoring *nul points* at the Eurovision song contest in 1970, yet Jean-Claude Juncker, the former Prime Minister of Luxembourg and newly-appointed President of the European Commission, may be the man who finally brings to an end the long-standing British ambivalence towards the EU. Ivan Rogers, the most senior UK diplomat in Brussels, certainly thinks so. During the controversy over Juncker's appointment, he warned that such a move could hasten Britain's exit. David Cameron fought against Juncker's appointment to the bitter end, but his failure only underlines the stark reality that the EU project was - and always will be - an attempt to merge the different nations into a federation – a new country called the "United States of Europe".

We in the UK have never liked the idea of sharing our sovereignty. In order to persuade us to join, the then Prime Minister, Edward Heath therefore had to resort to deceit. He told us that we would be leaving one free trade area, EFTA, to join another larger and more dynamic one. When the White Paper, *The United Kingdom and the European Communities*, was published in 1971, no mention was made of plans for economic or monetary union, nor the loss of sovereignty. In such circumstances, it is hardly surprising that opposition to our membership of the EEC (as it then was) has always been rumbling away in the background. When the Conservative government of Edward Heath was ousted by the Labour Party under Harold Wilson in 1974, the Labour manifesto had pledged to seek a fundamental renegotiation of our membership terms. This pledge eventually turned into an in/out referendum in 1975, where the electorate voted by two to one to stay in, even though very little was actually renegotiated. However, although we stayed in, we soon gained a reputation in

Brussels as the awkward partner - a reputation we have never succeeded in shaking off. In the 1970s, the strongest opposition to UK membership came from the left wing of the Labour Party. The late Tony Benn said, "I loathe the Common Market. It's bureaucratic and centralised, there's no political discussion. Officials control ministers and it just has a horrible flavour about it." Hugh Gaitskell, Wilson's predecessor as Labour leader and by no means a left-winger, had been strongly opposed to UK membership. In 1962, he made a speech expressing concern that joining the EEC would loosen the ties with the Commonwealth, warning that Britain would become a "province of Europe." These attitudes lingered in the Labour Party for years after his death. As recently as 1983, it fought a general election on a manifesto pledging to withdraw Britain from the Common Market. The Labour candidate for Sedgefield in Durham, a certain Anthony Blair, promised in his election address that "We'll negotiate for a withdrawal from the EEC, which has drained our natural resources and destroyed jobs." Had another referendum on withdrawal been held in this period, the outcome could have been very different from 1975.

Support for withdrawal from the EU has ebbed and flowed in the years between the 1980s and the early 2000s, but in the last few years it has built up a real head of steam that could well develop into an unstoppable momentum. The September 2013 *British Social Attitudes* survey indicated that a record 2 out of 3 people either wanted the UK to leave the EU altogether or wished for the EU's powers to be reduced. An opinion poll published in The Observer in June 2014 shows a substantial majority in favour of withdrawal if there is no substantial reform. We are fed up with the bossy bureaucrats of Brussels, with only a few individuals such as Roy Jenkins, the only Briton ever appointed President of the European Commission, being keen on losing our identity to become part of a United States of Europe.

Although "Europe" appears to be a fairly low priority for UK voters, being ranked in between 7th and 9th place in recent YouGov surveys of voters' concerns, EU legislation is a hidden element behind many issues ranked higher. Awareness of the EU angle to the second most important issue, immigration, is now widespread thanks to the publicity surrounding the lifting in January 2014 of restrictions on Bulgarian and Romanian migration to the UK. However, people often only become aware of the damaging effect of the EU in other areas if it has affected them personally – for instance, those who become victims of cashpoint fraud by Romanian criminal gangs or when a variety of plant, a pigment in paint, a pesticide, a type of fuel or some other commodity is suddenly removed from the shelf by some irritating EU directive.

Support for withdrawal would be higher had successive governments not sought to hide the damage done by the EU to our country. They have good reason for their deceit, for the more the electorate knows about the scale of interference by Brussels in our daily lives, the more apparent it becomes how powerless our own ministers have become to stop these unpopular directives being foisted upon us. Vivianne Reding, the EU's justice commissioner and vice-president of the European Commission, made a particularly stupid comment in February this year when she claimed that the British People were too ill-informed to vote in a referendum. "I don't care what kind of personal decision you take," she said. "The only thing I care for is that you take an informed decision, whatever your decision be." Given the level of support for withdrawal when a good many people are not yet aware of the aim to create a superstate nor the scale of EU meddling in the political process, if they were better informed (and this is one of the aims of this book), support for withdrawal would be even stronger.

Until recently, our relationship with the EU stood in marked contrast to those of our Continental neighbours. Even now, it is impossible to imagine Germany, Belgium or Italy ever holding a referendum to leave the EU. It seems bizarre to us that Greece, whose economic woes can be blamed solidly on the Euro, remains firmly committed not just to the EU but to the single currency too, while in 2012 the Croatian people voted to join the EU – in the midst of the Eurozone crisis! It is inconceivable that the UK would vote to join if we were considering accession now, rather than 42 years ago. Things are starting to change across the continent. Besides UKIP's success in the 2014 European Parliamentary elections, Marine le Pen's anti-EU *Front National* topped the poll in France while anti-immigration eurosceptic *Dansk Folkeparti* (Danish People's Party) won the largest share of the vote in Denmark. These results confirm the findings of a poll by Gallup Europe in September 2013 that only 30% of those surveyed viewed the EU positively compared to 70% 20 years ago. It concluded that "the European project has never in its history been so unpopular". An article in the Dutch newspaper *de Volkskrant*, written in the aftermath of May's elections, summarises the mood across the continent:- "The European idea, as developed since the Treaty of Maastricht, is the main victim of the elections. If you add the non-voters to the voters who have supported a europhobic or eurosceptic party, it's only one third of EU citizens which supports the European project. Apparently Europe, which is being shaped without the people and sometimes against the people, doesn't appeal any longer."

A crunch time is approaching for the UK, especially as the EU's priorities will increasingly revolve around the Eurozone. We became "semi-detached" from the EU over 20 years ago when we opted out of the Single Currency and it is inconceivable that we would ever wish to join now. Even before the recent financial problems faced by Greece, Portugal, Ireland and Spain, a majority of the UK public wished to keep the pound and the Eurozone crisis has hardened public attitudes still further. This means that if we do not withdraw from the EU, we shall soon find ourselves increasingly on the periphery. On 12th September 2012, José Manuel Barroso, the then President of the European Commission, delivered a "state of the Union" address where he reaffirmed the objective of the EU: "Let's not be afraid of the words: we shall need to move towards a federation of nation states. This is what we need. This is our political horizon." One of the lessons from the recent crisis, said Mr Barroso, is that a common currency requires a common fiscal policy, so the next major surrender of sovereignty by the member states will be the power to tax and spend. However, **this will only be required of the Eurozone**

countries. Along with other member states that still use national currencies, the UK will largely be on the outside of these developments.

What Barroso and others have in mind as the next step towards a federal Europe is a United States of Eurozone. The different nations who share the common currency are still far from united as to how to proceed, but a new treaty is likely to be formulated before long. Olli Rehn, the European Commissioner for Economic and Monetary Affairs, suggested in a speech on 19th February 2013 that "In the medium-term (18 months to 5 years), we could envisage further integration involving Treaty changes." At the October 2013 EU summit, the government leaders discussed a draft text which stated that "Work will be carried forward to strengthen economic policy coordination, including on the main features of contractual arrangements." Thanks to the Conservatives' "Referendum lock", if the UK government were asked to sign any new EU treaty, it would first be subject to a referendum. There is no likelihood of our backing a treaty surrendering more power to the EU; hence the reason why it will apply only to the Eurozone, which will then forge ahead with closer political union - including possibly establishing a separate Eurozone parliament - leaving the UK on the outside. Whatever the outcome, it is inevitable that the current relationship between our country and the rest of the EU will have to change.

These developments have been rumbling away in the background since the start of the Eurozone crisis and provide the backdrop for David Cameron's announcement on 23rd January last year committing a future Conservative government to renegotiating certain aspects of Britain's membership of the European Union if his party wins the 2015 General Election. The renegotiated package would then be put to a referendum by the British electorate, who will be asked whether the United Kingdom should remain a member of the European Union. Mr. Cameron has made it clear that he wishes the UK to remain a member of the EU, so if the referendum takes place, he will be campaigning for a "Yes" vote, as will the leaders of the Labour and Liberal Democrat parties, the BBC, many senior civil servants, and some leaders of big business.

It was over a year later before Cameron finally released any details of his "wish list" for the renegotiations. The seven points he hopes to discuss are as follows:-

1. Powers flowing away from Brussels, not always to it.
2. National parliaments able to work together to block "unwanted European legislation."
3. Businesses liberated from red tape and benefiting from the strength of the EU's own market to open up greater free trade with North America and Asia.
4. UK police forces and justice systems able to protect British citizens, unencumbered by unnecessary interference from the European institutions, including the European Court of Human Rights.
5. Free movement to take up work, not free benefits.
6. Support for the continued enlargement of the EU to new members but with new mechanisms in place to prevent vast migrations across the continent.
7. Ensuring Britain is no longer subject to the concept of "ever closer union", enshrined in the treaty, to which every EU country currently has to sign up.

There are four observations which can be made about this list. Firstly, some of the points are very vague. Secondly, Cameron's own ministers have supported measures in direct contradiction to some of these points. Thirdly, as we shall see, they only scratch the surface and do not address much of the fundamental damage already caused by the EU and finally, there is considerable doubt as to whether the leaders of the other member states, let alone the European Parliament, will be sympathetic. The idea of a "bespoke new deal" as championed by Business for Britain, which would enable the UK to remain within the EU on our own terms, looks to be a non-starter. Already, David Cameron has sparked outrage in Poland by suggesting limits on free movement of people, while the French government has already made clear its strong opposition to a "pick and mix" approach by the UK where we only submit to the legislation that suits us. Cameron's campaign against Jean-Claude Juncker has further alienated other EU leaders, making them less likely to be sympathetic to the UK. We are not popular in Brussels. Daniel Hannan, a British Conservative MEP described a debate in the European Parliament where "one after another, MEPs rose to jeer at the europhobia and the selfishness of the British…Our presence in the EU is the single most common cause of conflict with our neighbours." We already have more derogations (exemptions) from EU legislation than any other member state. José Manual Barroso recently said that the UK could be treated as "the special one," but how special? He dismissed of any attempt to hold a "fundamental discussion about the competences of the EU….in terms of renationalisation," adding that he thought this approach would be "doomed to failure…. There will be others, many, who oppose" the UK's (or any other nation's) repatriating powers from the EU. Among these opponents is the German Socialist party, the SPD, the junior partners in Germany's coalition government, who refuse to support any compromise on the EU's founding principle of "ever closer union." Manfred Weber, the new leader of the centre-right EPP faction in the European Parliament, made the same point, claiming that, "For us this, is non-negotiable. We cannot sell Europe's soul... If we grant each national parliament a veto right, Europe would come to a virtual standstill." The German Chancellor Angela Merkel, whose CDU party operates in close alliance with Weber's CSU, was keen to emphasise that all those hoping she would come out in support of fundamental reform of the EU's structures "are in for a disappointment" when she addressed Parliament in Westminster in February 2014.

So, in view of the extreme unlikelihood of any renegotiations achieving either a significant improvement in the relationship between the UK and the EU or a change in direction for the entire EU project, we are faced with two choices. We can either remain a square peg in a round hole, an uncomfortable member of a club seeking ever-closer union whose rules will be less and less in accord with our wishes, or else we can break free and leave. It ought to be blindingly obvious that independence is the better option, but scaremongering has caused many to hesitate. It would be an economic disaster, so europhile politicians like Nick Clegg tell us, with widespread job losses and a significant withdrawal of foreign investment. Given such dire warnings, it is hardly surprising that many people in favour of independence claim they would change their minds if a renegotiated membership were possible. In reality, any renegotiated deal will only scratch the surface. The EU will not change course so "out" will always be better than "in". Furthermore, "out" would provide a wonderful opportunity for a fresh start for the UK, with greater personal freedom, more money in our pockets and less red tape to strangle our businesses. Withdrawal is an exciting prospect. David Cameron should not be calling supporters of withdrawal pessimists. Regaining our independence offers the best opportunity finally to leave the dark days of recession and feeble growth behind. It is the complete opposite of the retreat into a narrow, nationalistic isolation of which europhiles accuse us. We are not "sleepwalking" towards the EU exit door as Ed Miliband fears. We are heading towards it with our eyes open in anticipation, thrilled at the thought of being masters of our own destiny once again.

However, the exit route will be long and hard. Although their arguments are weak, supporters of our continuing EU membership have considerable resources at this disposal and a long, hard battle must needs be fought to defeat them. There is no guarantee that a referendum will be held in 2017. At the moment, it will only take place if the Conservatives are returned to power in next year's general election. Labour has so far refused to commit itself to matching the Conservatives' pledge, in spite of a lacklustre performance in the European Parliamentary elections. Then, even if a referendum did take place, would the Prime Minister abide by the result, or will he (or she) go into a sulk and refuse to start negotiations?

Also, if we were to withdraw, how would we go about it, and what would be the shape of our new relationship with the EU? This book does not go into any detail on this last question, although readers wishing to pursue this matter further will find an excellent analysis of the different independence options in Robert Oulds' book *Everything you wanted to know about the EU but were too afraid to ask* (Bretwalda, 2014).

In writing this book, I have chosen to restrict its scope to a summary of the best reasons for withdrawal. It has been borne out of frustration that, notwithstanding the outstanding performance of UKIP in the 2014 European Parliamentary elections, some opinion polls still suggest that the majority of the electorate still want our country to remain shackled to the EU. Given that the arguments in support of independence are so strong, more informed voices to present the case are urgently needed, so that we do indeed vote for withdrawal when that crucial referendum comes. I say "when" rather than "if" in spite of Labour dragging its feet. Even if Labour is returned to power next year without having committed itself to holding a vote on our EU membership, the desire among the British people to have their say will not go away. Defeat for David Cameron would almost certainly be followed by one of two positive outcomes – his replacement as Tory leader by a convinced withdrawalist or a split within the Conservative Party with the majority of its membership and its better MPs joining forces with the UKIP rank and file to create a party pledged to take Britain out. Given that a Miliband-led government is likely to see its popularity plunge as quickly and as dramatically as that of François Hollande's socialists in France, the new withdrawalist party could well find itself in power in the next general election after May 2015, by which time the argument in favour of withdrawal will have been all but won, assuming the EU itself has not imploded by then in the wake of a renewed crisis within the Eurozone.

I cannot claim that this book is a pioneering work. It has drawn on the work of a number of earlier researchers and writers who have already made the case for British withdrawal. However, many of their books and papers either deal with just one or two of the subjects covered here, or else go into perhaps too much technical detail for the average reader, I therefore believe this book has a useful role to perform in setting out all the main arguments for withdrawal clearly and concisely, without leaving the reader bogged down in a mass of statistics. My hope is that we do not repeat the mistake of the 1975 referendum and allow ourselves to be fobbed off with a token repatriation of a few insignificant powers. Our destiny is to be a free nation again, active on the world stage as a player in our own right. We must grasp with both hands this once-in-a-lifetime opportunity to bring it about.

Chapter 1
We can be masters in our own house

Dear Reader, do you like being bossed around by foreigners? Are you comfortable with foreign politicians and bureaucrats being able to impose their will on our parliament? You probably aren't and you shouldn't be ashamed to admit it either. No successful nation normally submits to rule from overseas unless it has been invaded.

Given that we have been blessed with over 900 years free from foreign invasion - in spite of the best efforts of Philip II of Spain, Napoleon and Hitler - it is hardly surprising that we in the UK feel particularly strongly about this subject. True, along with the rest of Western Europe, we were subject to the Papacy during the Middle Ages, but here too, the foreign yoke was broken many years ago – in this case by Henry VIII in 1534."The Bishop of Rome hath no jurisdiction in this Realm of England" says Article XXXVII of the Church of England's 39 Articles – an early expression of our deeply-ingrained hostility to foreign interference in our country's affairs. The Sun newspaper recently expressed this same sentiment in a somewhat less polite manner with its famous 1990 headline *Up Yours, Delors* and its accompanying V-sign, showing in no uncertain terms what it thought of the then President of the European Commission and his vision of a federal Europe. Ralph Miliband, father of the present leader of the Labour Party, noted the strong love we have for our country and its institutions shortly after arriving as a teenage refugee from Belgium during the Second World War. "The Englishman is a rabid nationalist. They are perhaps the most nationalist people in the world", he wrote. We've had to suffer some pretty rotten rulers over the centuries from Edward II to Edward Heath and at different times have invited both Dutch and German princes to become our king, but in the main we have done very well as an independent, self-governing country. Why shouldn't we oppose the idea of sharing (or "pooling") our sovereignty with 27 other nations? On the face of it, it's a pretty daft idea.

Most other successful nations think so too. There are other regional trading blocs elsewhere in the world - such as the Association of South East Asian Nations (ASEAN) and the South American Common Market MERCOSUR, but the members of these trading blocs are independent, self-governing nations, even though in the case of MERCOSUR, most of its members have far more in common with each other than the 28 members of the EU - sharing a history of colonisation by Spain and a common language. Indeed, there are plenty of other nations in the world which share a common culture and language and which are relatively close to one another geographically, but which have never felt any need to "pool" their sovereignty. For instance, New Zealand and Australia, which were both settled by the British, speak English and based their legal systems on English Common Law. Even though New Zealand boasts a population of less than 4½ million people, it has not felt the need to share its sovereignty, let alone merge, with its larger neighbour. Likewise Canada and the USA are happy to associate with each other (and Mexico) through NAFTA, the North American Free Trade Area, but have no desire to share their sovereignty either. Closer to home is Norway, which rejected membership of the EU in 1972 and again in 1994. Its history as a nation goes back many centuries, albeit closely linked to its neighbours Denmark and Sweden. Not only do the peoples of these countries look very similar and speak similar languages, but they have shared their sovereignty in the past. All three nations were united under one ruler between 1388 and 1521 and after this date, Norway was ruled first by Denmark then by Sweden, only regaining its independence in 1905, after over 500 years. Denmark and Sweden are once again sharing their sovereignty, not just with each other but with the 26 other member states of the European Union. Norway, however, has been happy not to follow suit. It has managed very successfully as an independent nation.

The desire for a nation to be self-governing is very natural and understandable. In the 1950s and 1960s, many former British and French colonies in Africa sought independence. They did not want to "pool" their sovereignty with the former colonial power, nor with each other. Many Tibetans, particularly among the diaspora in the UK and the USA, seek their homeland's independence from China, although regrettably our spineless Prime Minister does not support their legitimate aspirations, presumably out of fear of offending the mighty People's Republic. The desire of the Catalans in Spain (or indeed the SNP in Scotland) to seek independence but stay subject to EU control is very weird when viewed in this context. For all its faults, at least Sinn Féin (which translates as "we ourselves") is more consistent: having sought for many years to create an united Ireland free from British control, it does not take too kindly to subjection to Brussels. Although not an outright withdrawalist party like UKIP, Sinn Féin has opposed every EU treaty in the referendums held in the Irish Republic. Its MEPs sit in the European Parliament as part of the Nordic Green Left group, which opposes most EU policy.

The closest parallel to the EU is the African Union (AU), which replaced the Organisation of African Unity in 2001 and which has similar institutions to its European counterpart, such as a Commission, a Pan-African Parliament and the Assembly of the African Union (which corresponds to the European Council.). While the AU's stated aim is to mimic other areas of the EU, including setting up a human rights court, a central bank and a single currency by 2023, the most enthusiastic advocate of a "United States of Africa," Libya's Colonel Gaddafi, was killed in 2011. Other African leaders, notably Yoweri Museveni, of Uganda, are less enthusiastic, preferring more economic integration to political union. Museveni feels Africa is too diverse to be under one government, although he, along with the leaders of over 50 other African states, signed the Accra Declaration in 2007, which states that the leaders are "convinced that the ultimate objective of the African Union is the United States of Africa with a union government."

It is significant that Africa is the continent which has been the keenest to replicate the EU model. Post-colonial Africa has not been the success story that supporters of the independence movements hoped for. Dictators such as Idi Amin in Uganda, Robert Mugabe in Zimbabwe and General Mobutu in Congo (Zaire) have caused much suffering among their countrymen. Somalia, without any effective government for two decades, is one of the worst examples in the world of a "failed state". Tribal and religious conflicts have led to violence and bloodshed in Rwanda, Nigeria, Sudan, Kenya and elsewhere. Poverty is widespread and in many African countries, democracy is still a dream. Significantly, few African states are ethnically homogeneous. The co-existence of diverse languages and cultures does little to foster a sense of unity and build a strong democratic nation state.

Herein lies the clue as to why the other 27 countries of the European Union don't feel as strongly about self-government as we do. Many of their citizens do not have the same pride in their country, its history and its democratic institutions as we have. At the time of UK accession - a mere 41 years ago - less than half of these member states were able to enjoy the freedoms that generations of Britons have taken for granted. Behind the Iron Curtain, hard-line Marxist régimes stifled any form of dissent, while Spain, Portugal and Greece were ruled by unelected dictators. This period was the tail-end of centuries of turmoil on the European mainland, an age when wars were endemic and national boundaries in a constant state of flux. Even in these more peaceful times ethnic and political boundaries do not always coincide. To take just a few examples, ethnic Hungarians can be found in substantial numbers in Romania and Slovakia, while Finland includes a Swedish-speaking minority. Belgium contains French speakers who are not French citizens, Dutch speakers who are not Dutch citizens and a small enclave of German speakers who are not German citizens. Meanwhile, the Basques, with their distinct language and culture, have no nation state of their own. Furthermore, the majority of the other 27 member states were at some stage in their history either part of the Holy Roman, Ottoman or Hapsburg empires or forced into an international federation such as Yugoslavia or the Soviet Union.

The European Union as an institution is actually quite proud of Europe's multi-national empires - well, some of them - in spite of the rather unsavoury individuals who founded them. Every year since 1950 in the German city of Aachen, a prize has been awarded to an individual in recognition of their "Distinguished service on behalf of European unification." The prize is named after Charlemagne, the first Holy Roman Emperor, who ruled over much of modern France, along with parts of Germany and Italy. The EU chooses to turn a blind eye to the brutal method he used to build his empire. He did not deal kindly with his subject peoples, forcing the conquered Saxons to choose between forced baptism or death. Yet even Pope John Paul II, who received the Charlemagne prize in 2004, overlooked his cruelty, affirming him uncritically as the "Father of Europe" in his acceptance speech.

The legacy of mainland European history is a mindset considerably less hostile to shared sovereignty than ours. Even though the latest survey in the EU's own *Eurobarometer* series suggests that for every person who trusts the EU, there are two who don't, withdrawal hasn't been discussed in any other member state to the same degree as in the UK – if at all. The reasons are varied. In the Baltic states of Estonia, Latvia and Lithuania, their loss of national identity following their enforced incorporation into the Soviet Union will linger in the people's minds for many years yet. For these small countries, sharing their sovereignty with other western European nations is viewed as an insurance policy worth paying in order to reduce the risk of any future Russian designs on their territory, a concern highlighted by recent events in Ukraine. Spain, Portugal and Greece would not want to walk away from an institution which they symbolically joined to prove that they had moved on from totalitarian dictatorships to join the family of democratic nations. France, after suffering German troops on its soil on three occasions between 1870 and 1945, would rather share sovereignty with Germany than face a fourth invasion.

Indeed, the European project gained much impetus in the aftermath of the Second World War. In those years, there was an understandable desire to bring these all-too frequent European conflicts finally to an end. Winston Churchill, the British Prime Minister during the war years, spoke at Zurich in 1946 about the need to "build a United States of Europe", by bringing to an end the "frightful nationalistic quarrels originated by the Teutonic nations" so that the nations of Europe might "regain the simple joys and hopes which make life worth living."

However, he was adamant that our country was to act as a midwife, helping to bring this new structure into being, rather than being a member of it. As long ago as 1930, when the idea of a European Federal Union was widely being discussed, he said, "We are with Europe but not of it. We are linked but not comprised. We are interested and associated but not absorbed....We must build a kind of United States of Europe. Great Britain, the British Commonwealth of Nations, mighty America must be friends and sponsors of the new Europe." Churchill never changed his mind. He later told France's General de Gaulle, "Each time Britain must choose between Europe and the open sea, we shall always choose the open sea."

Of course, the world has moved on since Winston Churchill made these speeches, but successful nation states are still thriving in 2014. There is no reason why the UK should not re-join their number. The nation state, especially one which incorporates a robust, well-established democratic process, encourages limited, accountable government. It acts as a brake on tyranny and fosters a sense of community. By contrast, multi-national federations, empires and superstates, especially when created without popular consent, tend to be remote, unstable and undemocratic. They have to be held together by large unaccountable bureaucracies, rarely last long and all too frequently leave behind a legacy of economic misery and violence. There is therefore no truth in the accusations made by supporters of the EU that those of us who seek the restoration of our national sovereignty are misty-eyed romantics trying to put the clock back. We have simply studied our history books and ponder the future of the European project with grave misgivings. Unfortunately, europhiles tend to be terribly self-righteous and dismiss these legitimate concerns contemptuously. Shortly before the German federal elections in September 2013, Wolfgang Schäuble, the country's finance minister, described the German anti-Euro party Alternative für Deutschland (AfD) as "people who seem to be trapped in the past." This is a pretty harsh criticism of a party which merely wants to reform the EU. It does not advocate German withdrawal. It is hardly extreme to believe that the single currency isn't viable in its present form. Plenty of serious economists inside and outside the EU have expressed similar opinions. Sadly, Schäuble's comments are typical of pro-Europeans. The European Council President, Herman van Rompuy, was no less forthright: "We have together to fight the danger of a new euroscepticism. The biggest enemy of Europe today is fear. Fear leads to egoism, egoism leads to nationalism and nationalism leads to war."

While we should be grateful for the peace that Europe has enjoyed since 1945, it flies in the face of reality to give the credit to the European Union. There is no conclusive proof that a group of sovereign nations with their own governments, languages and customs will inevitably end up at war with each other. Maybe Europe's track record between the end of the Roman Empire and 1945 has not been very impressive on this front, but the establishment of democracy within a nation has proved a far more effective way of preventing a war than pooling sovereignty. There is no current hint a potential war between any member states of the EU, but it is no guarantor of peace. The Eurozone crisis has not only increased tensions between the Northern and Southern nations but, according to a 2013 report commissioned by the International Labour Organisation, has resulted in a number of EU member states facing a serious risk of civil unrest.

In summary, self-government is the norm across the globe for successful nations. The pooled sovereignty of the EU is a weird abnormality. The EU is quite unapologetic about its abnormality. For instance it has emblazoned these words on the wall in the EU Parliament's Visitors Centre:- **"National sovereignty is the root**

cause of the most crying evils of our times...The only final remedy for this supreme and catastrophic evil of our time is a federal union of the peoples", but this does not make its attitude any the less abnormal. It is an unfortunate hangover from the post-war period when it was widely felt across the European mainland that the nation state was a failed concept which caused conflict – a sentiment which never caught on in the UK. The idea that the UK should govern itself once again is therefore just simple common sense – neither right wing nor left wing. We fully sympathise with our European neighbours' desire to avoid another war, but they must recognise that our desire to regain our sovereignty is perfectly natural, even if the very possibility is already upsetting some of them. Take, for example, Frank-Walter Steinmeyer, the German foreign minister, who recently claimed that the biggest threat to peace comes from eurosceptic parties like UKIP. What is he implying? That Nigel Farage's party must be held in check to prevent a convoy of German tanks crossing the Rhine? Get real! Equally paranoid is the former Italian Prime Minister Enrico Letta, who recently called UK withdrawal a "real threat" while at the same time insisting that, "we need integrated governance." Sorry, Signor Letta, but like most of the rest of the world, we don't want integrated governance. That's precisely why we have never felt happy within the EU. If you don't think your country is capable of managing its own affairs or of remaining at peace with its neighbours without integrated governance, that's fine, but we are not so pessimistic about ours, even if our current political leadership leaves a lot to be desired. Maybe a UK exit would cause a big upset within the EU; maybe it might even lead to a "domino effect," with other countries thinking about following us through the exit door, but that's not our problem. For us, there is everything to be gained by withdrawal; we have nothing to lose but our chains.

Chapter 2: The restoration of our ancient liberties

Any UK citizen who visits Saudi Arabia, Iran or Qatar for the first time will soon discover that the legal systems of these lands are very different from ours. While there are different schools of Islamic or Sharia Law, in each of these countries, the net result is a very obviously different "feel" to the UK. By contrast, it may not seem obvious if we cross the channel to France or Belgium that these countries also have a very different legal system from that which evolved in our country over many centuries. The people in these countries look and behave in a similar fashion to us. Like us, they enjoy legal protection from torture or slavery; they do not face amputation of their limbs for theft; they have the freedom to change their religion or not to practise any religion at all. However, beneath these apparent similarities are some very real differences, which are of great importance as far as the future relationship of our country to the European Union is concerned. Dear Reader, you might have felt tempted to skip this chapter because the sight of the words "legal system" could make you concerned that you will be lost in a mass of technical jargon that will go over your head. If so, please think again and read on. Your author is no trained lawyer, and the concepts at the heart of this chapter are actually quite simple and have profound implications if you value your freedom.

We the people.....

In the previous chapter we considered how it is natural for any successful self-respecting nation to wish to govern itself and not be imposed upon by any foreign power. Currently, the UK has not just lost that freedom, but it has lost it to a group of nations whose attachment to freedom runs nowhere near as deep as does ours. It is hard to ascertain how our attachment to freedom began, but our excellent legal system, known as Common Law, certainly played its part. Its origins are lost in the mists of time, but the Saxon and Viking invaders who occupied Britain in the centuries after the Roman legions withdrew in 410 AD probably brought it with them. It insists that **government rests on the consent of the governed** – in other words, rulers are accountable to their subjects. The American legal scholar J. Reuben Clark Jr. (1871-1961) highlighted its virtues: *"The sovereign power in a Common Law system rests exclusively with the people. Individual rights, by extension, become a fact of daily life that cannot be breached by an aspiring tyrant without bloody consequences. Over time, this system of judge-made law allows for the gradual development of an organic legal framework whilst minimising encroachments upon individual rights."* Common Law's insistence that rulers only rule by the consent of the people has clipped the wings of several monarchs who tried to flout the system. King John, for instance, was humbled by his barons when he taxed them too much. They rebelled against him and forced him to sign a document which they claimed would re-establish "the ancient liberty of church and kingdom." This document - the Magna Carta – or "great charter of the liberties of the people" laid the foundations of Parliamentary democracy as far back as 1215. Power ultimately rests with the people, even though they choose representatives in a parliamentary election to speak up on their behalf to the ruler, or rulers. This principle still stands in theory, even though many of our MPs today now sadly ignore their accountability to the electorate, placing greater importance on the orders of their whips or the favour of their party leader than the opinions of their constituents. Indeed, the signing of the European Communities Act, 1972, which surrendered our sovereignty to that of the European Economic Community, was the most appalling betrayal of the people by elected politicians in the entire history of our country.

...versus the supremacy of the state

By contrast, most continental legal systems are based on civil law. While there are many differences between, say, French and German law, all civil law-based legal codes owe much to Napoleon's law code, which in turn was based on Roman law. Under these systems, again to quote J. Reuben Clark: "The sovereign power rested in the head of the state, who granted to the people, his subjects, the rights he decided they should have, reserving any other rights in himself, as likewise the right to extend, alter, add to, or withdraw these rights already granted." In other words, continental law is a top-down system where the state, be it an absolute monarch like an ancient Roman emperor, or the government of a modern country like France or Germany, is the ultimate source of power, granting only such freedoms to the people as it deems fit. A change of ruler can therefore mean a change in the boundaries of freedom. The concept of inalienable liberties that no ruler can take away is unknown across most of the Continent. Civil law reigns supreme in the other member states except for Cyprus, Malta and the Irish Republic, all of which were administered by the UK at some time in their history. Its top-down mentality therefore colours the mindset of the European Union institutions as a whole. When the Danes rejected the Maastricht Treaty in a referendum in 1992, they were made to vote again the following year as they had delivered the "wrong" result, as were the Irish when they voted against the Lisbon Treaty in 2008. By the EU's own rules, the Irish result should have killed Lisbon dead, as it required the signature of all 27 member states. However, the will of people could not be allowed to derail the great European project! Ireland, in spite of its Common Law foundation, was small enough to bully. No wonder the EU élite was keen to ensure that the UK, whose electorate would have insisted that "no" meant "no," was not granted a referendum, Unfortunately, the spineless Gordon Brown was all too willing to oblige, even though Labour had promised in its 2005 manifesto to hold a referendum on the European Constitution, which everyone else in Europe apart from our government admitted was to all intents and purposes identical with the Lisbon Treaty which replaced it.

The fiasco over these referendum results, along with the rejection of the European Constitution by voters in France and the Netherlands in 2005, illustrates only too well the sheer folly of our being unequally yoked to an institution dominated by men from countries with a long, legally-established tradition of top-down government. It certainly does not serve the interests of our country, and also encroaches on our liberties.

There are many other examples which can be quoted to prove these points, but space permits mention of only a few.

A surfeit of regulation

When power rests with the people, regulation will usually only be enacted where necessary and with a reasonable degree of popular support. For example, in the 19th century, the banning of child labour in the coal mines and spinning mills came about because reformers like Lord Shaftesbury managed to build a consensus among informed opinion that it was morally wrong. The ensuing Factory Acts therefore came about because Parliament had to reflect the will of the people. By contrast, when ultimate power rests with the state, legislation can be (and in the case of the EU, is) introduced to address issues which from a UK perspective do not appear to require any legislation whatsoever. In 2003, the tar-based insecticide Mortegg disappeared from the shelves. It had been used by fruit growers since at least 1925 to kill over-wintering bugs. It worked successfully and caused no side effects, except to leave a lingering smell of tar on the person doing the spraying. However, the EU in its wisdom decided to ban it and its replacement has not proved so effective. Thousands of similar examples of pointless legislation could be quoted. One of the most bizarre is Commission Regulation (EC) No. 1462/2006, which purports to concern "the classification of certain goods in the Combined Nomenclature." After a tedious preamble about various Council regulations, it turns out that this document, which would have been translated into at least 20 languages, concerns the tariff classification of – can you believe it – a cuddly toy sheep! See image opposite.

Almost as daft and more widely known is Commission Regulation 2257/94 - the so-called "straight banana directive." It does indeed insist that the bananas must be "without bending," although this is probably an example of bad translation from another language – after all, even the European Commission cannot be so stupid as to believe that all bananas must be straight! However, there is no ambiguity about the absurd level of detail about the permitted number of bananas in a bunch, or the insistence that the word "Bananas" must appear on the packaging if no actual fruits are visible. (Anyone wishing to check this out should look up http://eur-lex.europa.eu/LexUriServ/LexUriServ.do?uri=CELEX:31994R2257:EN:HTML and see if they can read it through to the end without falling asleep in sheer boredom.) Our country had been importing bananas from the Caribbean for many years previously without the slightest demand for rubbish like this to be put on the statute books.

We will return to the subject of regulation in the next chapter. It is a vast subject, but our instinctive anger about such nonsense is well founded. However, the labelling of bananas and the tariff classification of cuddly toys are minor issues compared to those to be considered below. A legal system founded on the supremacy of the state does not act in our interest - even in theory.

Policing

A British policeman may appear to exercise a similar function to a continental gendarme, but there are some profound differences, which again go back to the different concepts behind the legal systems. As Christopher Gill, one of the former "Maastricht Rebel" Conservative MPs explains, "The tradition of British policing has been to protect individuals and their property from criminal activity and to apprehend those who transgress whereas on the continent police act almost like an army of occupation, responsible for public order enforcement, crowd control and generally buttressing the authority of the civil state as opposed to defending the freedom of the individual citizen". In our country, the police are, in theory, on our side, to work on our behalf and deriving their authority from us, whereas continental police are an extension of the state. It is hardly surprising that, when EUGENDFOR – a pan-European Gendarmerie - was established, the UK government initially wanted nothing to do with it. Sadly, in 2013, this wise principle was compromised, and a limited authorisation was granted for foreign police to operate in the UK. Admittedly, as Christopher Gill pointed out, "these foreign police will not be permitted to carry firearms while on British soil and will only be allowed to remain here for a maximum of five hours in pursuit of a suspect," but why? Our own police are perfectly competent to tackle foreign criminals operating in this country. We are right to be suspicious, especially when "officers of the House of Commons refuse to allow MPs to table questions seeking a categorical assurance from Government Ministers that the European Gendarmerie will never be deployed on British soil.".

European Arrest Warrant and other horrors

Besides the worrying arrival of continental police in this country, the European Arrest Warrant (EAW) is another dangerous impingement on our liberties. No one would deny that, with criminals able to cross national boundaries with relative ease, some form of international co-operation between police forces is essential, but the European Arrest Warrant is not the answer. In the summer of 2013, Theresa May, the Home Secretary, announced that the UK would opt out of all 133 law and order measures included in the Lisbon Treaty, but then stated her desire to opt back into 35 of them, including DNA sharing and the EAW. Although this "opt-in" has the support of some senior policemen, it would be a big mistake for two reasons. Firstly, it would surrender the ultimate authority in cases of law to foreign judges at the European Court of Justice in Strasbourg and secondly, it would allow UK citizens to be extradited to another country and charged for an offence that is not a crime in our country. We cannot be confident that the legal process in some other EU member states operates to the standards to which we have been accustomed, even though the presumption of innocence is written into the Charter of Fundamental Rights of the European Union (see below). Readers may recall the 12 innocent British aircraft spotters arrested in Greece in 2001 on a charge of spying. The EAW increases the possibility of incidents like these. In 2007, a woman called Deborah Dark was arrested at gunpoint while on holiday in Turkey, as the French authorities had issued an EAW seeking her extradition on drug smuggling charges, of which she had been acquitted 18 years earlier. She was released and returned to the UK, but although Westminster magistrates refused a subsequent extradition request from France, believing there was no case to answer, she could face rearrest if ever she travelled on the Continent.

Because relatively few people in this country end up in court accused of a crime, most of us are unaware of the safeguards in our legal system which protect us against false accusation, arbitrary arrest and wrongful imprisonment; safeguards which are absent on most of the continent and thus absent for any UK citizen charged under a European Arrest Warrant. Under Common Law, defendants have a right to silence. No one may be tried in absentia – in other words without being present in court. Press coverage is restricted when a case is sub judice so as not to prejudice a fair trial. Most importantly, except where terrorism is involved, any person who is arrested must be charged in open court within 24 hours of arrest. Crucially, the 'charge' has to be backed by prima facie evidence as opposed to hearsay. Even when the suspect is thought to have committed murder, detention without charge may only be extended, with the permission of magistrates, to a maximum of 96 hours.

Given that these safeguards often do not exist on the continent, it is possible for a UK citizen to be tried in another EU state without being present at the trial or even knowing that the trial is taking place, convicted on hearsay evidence and then surrendered by the UK authorities if an EAW is issued. It is a frightening scenario, as several UK citizens have already discovered. Even the presumption of innocence enshrined in the EU's Charter of Fundamental Rights cannot be taken for granted. Andrew Symeou, a UK citizen, was extradited to Greece, denied bail and incarcerated for 11 months on homicide charges thanks to the signature of a Greek magistrate that no UK judge could overturn despite the evidence against him being obtained under duress. Edmond Arapi was subject to an Italian EAW in 2004, being convicted in absentia of a murder in Genoa, even though he had never visited Genoa in his life and was working in a café in Staffordshire on the day of the murder. Things could get worse. One of the very first actions taken in 2010 by Theresa May when she became Home Secretary was to opt into the planned European Investigation Order, thereby removing any right to opt out later. When enacted, this measure is intended to give foreign courts and prosecutors the power to order the British police to investigate, search, interrogate and gather evidence against British citizens; as well as to put us under surveillance, tap communications, monitor bank accounts and take DNA samples and other biometric data. The only way out of this dangerous impingement on our liberties is for us to leave the EU. Only thus can our police once again be the protectors of our liberties. They are currently slowly being converted into the agents of a foreign state. It is absurd for David Cameron to talk of renegotiating our relationship with the EU so that "UK police forces and justice systems are able to protect British citizens, unencumbered by unnecessary interference from the European institutions" when his Home Secretary is pursuing a totally opposite course. Ironically, our best chance of keeping our opt-out from the EAW could be the refusal of other member states, notably France and Spain, to allow us to apply a "proportionality" test, which enables us to reject EAWs for what are regarded in this country as trivial incidents.

The ECJ and the ECHR

Any discussion of law and liberty needs to clarify the difference between these two courts, as some readers may be confused on this issue. The European Court of Justice, established in 1963 and based in Luxembourg, is a European Union institution, whereas the Strasbourg-based European Court of Human Rights is an institution of the Council of Europe. The Council of Europe shares the same flag as the EU – the so-called "ring of death" – and also exists to promote European integration. However, it is a separate organisation which, unlike the EU, cannot pass binding laws and does not require its member states to transfer any sovereignty. The Council of Europe drafted the European Convention on Human Rights as early as 1960, although it was not incorporated into UK law until 1998, through the Human Rights Act, even though the UK was one of its founding members. One reason for the long delay was the reservations felt particularly by some Conservative MPs that it would result in a replacement of the older common-sense UK concept of human rights with a more politically correct variant. Their reservations have proved well-founded. It has been the ECHR appeals system which delayed the deportation of the extremist Moslem cleric Abu Qatada by 10 years and the ECHR which is insisting that the UK ends its blanket ban on prisoners being allowed to vote. Some leading Conservatives have talked of including a widespread re-vamp of human rights legislation or even withdrawal from the ECHR in their next election manifesto. It must be conceded that some individuals have been vindicated by the ECHR following some very silly decisions from the UK judiciary. Nadia Eweida, a Christian who was banned from wearing a cross by her employee, British Airways, saw the verdict overturned by judges in Strasbourg after failing to win her case in our courts. However, such positive decisions are rare. Three other Christians who appealed to the ECHR on religious discrimination issues at the same time all lost their cases. Even the odd successful appeal such as Mrs Eweida's poses the question as to whether foreigners should be allowed to interfere with the UK's legal system. In the 14th century, the three Acts of Praemunire (1353, 1365 and 1393) were passed, which made it a criminal offence to appeal to or obey a foreign court. These laws remained on the statute books for centuries without anyone seeing the need to repeal them. This is unsurprising, as such legislation is a common-sense application of the principle of being a self-governing nation. Praemunire was finally repealed in 1967 in the run-up to joining the European Economic Community. We now have to be subservient to foreign courts in certain areas, like it or not. Indeed, foreign courts can overrule not only the UK judiciary but the UK parliament. Lord Neuberger, the president of the UK Supreme Court was right to express his disgust at this state of affairs."The idea of courts overruling decisions of the UK parliament, as is substantially the effect of what the Strasbourg and the Luxembourg courts can do, is little short of offensive to our notions of constitutional propriety", he said.

Can these appalling developments be reversed? In particular, is the proposal to pull out of the ECHR any more than empty rhetoric? Some officials have suggested that such a move would require the UK to withdraw from the Council of Europe and Nigel Farage, UKIP's leader, claims that Vivianne Reding, the former EU justice commissioner, made it clear that while we are part of the EU, the UK **must** be a signatory of the ECHR and implement its decisions. In other words, withdrawal from the ECHR would require not just withdrawal from the Council of Europe but withdrawal from the EU. Another UKIP MEP, Gerard Batten, wrote to David Cameron in 2011 pointing out that the proposal then under discussion for the EU to accede to the European Convention on Human Rights in its own right required a unanimous decision of the European Council (Heads of Government), which was meeting at that time. Britain had a veto and

Mr Cameron could stop the accession by simply saying 'No'. Mr Batten was concerned that if the EU acceded to the ECHR as an institution on its own behalf, it would mean that all the member states would automatically be subject to it. He received a reply from Lord McNally on the Government's behalf, saying that because accession to the ECHR was in the Lisbon Treaty, the Government could not oppose it "as a matter of principle". Lord McNally then went on to say that the EU's own accession would not make any difference. If this sounds confusing, things would have been clearer if David Cameron had exercised his veto. Sadly, in his usual duplicitous way, he chose not to, while subsequently allowing his MPs to engage in much empty rhetoric.

Withdrawal from the EU is most definitely required to free ourselves from the ECJ, the European Union institution responsible, among other things, for fining EU member states for failure to obey EU law. The National Audit Office stated in January 2011 that Britain had already paid out £398 million and another £601 million was being set aside in anticipation of further fines – a grand total of approximately £1 billion. Some of the fines are totally pathetic. For instance, the National Museum of Labour History in Manchester was fined £7,223 by the ECJ just for failing to display a representation of the EU flag on a billboard. A country with our great history of liberty should not have to put up with being kicked around by a foreign judiciary in this way.

More significantly, the ECJ acts as the enforcer of another piece of human rights legislation, this time created by the European Union – the Charter of Fundamental Rights of the EU. At the time the Lisbon Treaty was signed, the former Prime Minister Tony Blair - an even more slippery character than David Cameron - told Parliament at the time that Britain had secured an opt-out in response to concerns about the impact on British justice. "It is absolutely clear that we have an opt-out from both the charter and judicial and home affairs. Those were the reasons why people like the Right Hon. Gentleman were saying that they wanted a referendum", he told Parliament on 25th June 2007. However, if there was really an opt-out, it has proved paper thin. In a series of rulings, the European Court of Justice has drawn explicitly on the Charter to force its decisions on Britain. Some of these decisions had vast consequences. For example, the ECJ cited the Charter when it banned cheaper car insurance for women (and cheaper annuities for men) on grounds of gender discrimination.

The country's top judges, who trusted Blair's assurance of an opt-out, were taken by surprise. Recently, Mr. Justice Mostyn told the High Court that a ruling in Luxembourg had now permanently extended the reach of human rights legislation in Britain. He added that the "constitutional significance of this decision can hardly be overstated...The Charter of Fundamental Rights of the European Union contains, I believe, all of those missing parts and a great deal more. Moreover, that the much wider Charter of Rights would remain part of our domestic law even if the Human Rights Act were repealed."

There is no need to go into further detail on either of these Charters. Both are based on a flawed understanding of human rights, based on the Continental concept of state supremacy, granting such rights as seems fit. Neither will guarantee an individual's inalienable rights as our Common Law system has done for centuries. It is therefore dangerous for our politicians to put the control of our criminal justice system beyond the control of UK courts or Parliament.

Even if we are to take David Cameron at his word when he talks about his desire that UK police forces and justice systems must be able to protect British citizens, unencumbered by unnecessary interference from the European institutions, he is not going anywhere near far enough. **Total repatriation of criminal justice to the member states is not on the agenda for renegotiation**, which it ought to be. Indeed, as Dominic Grieve, the former Attorney General, recently pointed out, the EU is breaking its own rules in an attempt to seize further powers from our justice system. Its Supreme Court, the ECJ, is not a court to dispense justice, as we understand the role of a court to be, but a political court, constituted to further the aims of the EU. If we value our liberty, this alone ought to be sufficient to encourage us to vote to withdraw from the EU in any forthcoming referendum. Only thus can we extricate ourselves from these developments. The EU is working towards the goal of a harmonised legal system, and it will be our Common Law, with its historic freedoms, which will ultimately have to give way. Lord Denning, the former Master of the Rolls (the second most senior judge in the UK), saw the danger as far back as 1990. "Our sovereignty has been taken away by the European Court of Justice.... Our courts must no longer enforce our national laws. They must enforce Community law... No longer is European law an incoming tide flowing up the estuaries of England. It is now like a tidal wave bringing down our sea walls and flowing inland over our fields and houses – to the dismay of all." As this chapter has shown, things have become worse since he wrote these words and there is more in the pipeline. Plans for a European Public Prosecutor (EPP) go back to the 1990s as part of a proposal to address budgetary fraud in the European Union. Under this proposal, the EPP would operate under a European legal framework based on the civil law principle and applicable in all member states. Even at the time, the setting up of a mechanism just to prosecute individuals for one specific class of offences was seen, in a consultation document dating from 1997 as "the embryo of a future European criminal code." In other words, it was to be the first step in the harmonisation of legal systems across the member states. Although more than 16 years have elapsed and the office of the EPP has yet to be established, it is still very much a live issue. Authority for its establishment was included in the Lisbon Treaty. The argument that an EU-wide legal system is necessary to deal with cross-border crime is not sufficient to warrant the erosion of our ancient liberties. For the good of our children and our children's children, we must withdraw from the EU.

Chapter 3
We could free ourselves from unnecessary and damaging legislation.

The origins and purpose of the European Commission

Why has a successful country with a long history of democracy fallen so low? We are now bossed around by foreigners and, what is worse, many of these foreigners have never been elected to their position of authority and cannot be removed by the ballot box. How did we end up in this sad state? In order to answer this question, we need to take a brief look at the history of the European project and the objectives behind it.

Charlemagne, the first Holy Roman Emperor, was mentioned briefly in Chapter 1. His empire, which included much of modern France, Germany and Italy, fell apart soon after his death in 814 AD. However, it inspired other continental rulers, notably Napoleon 1,000 years later, to copy his example and attempt to unite the nations of the European mainland into a single state. In Napoleon's day, the country that is now Germany comprised a number of independent states, each with its own ruler. Under the leadership of Prussia, the most powerful state, the smaller states were gradually absorbed and the German nation state finally came into being in 1871. The emergence of this powerful country was to alter the historic balance of power between the older established European states and, in brief, resulted in two catastrophic world wars.

Many questions were asked in the aftermath of the First World War as to how to avoid a repeat of such appalling carnage. The prevailing answer given, particularly by left-wing intellectuals across the continent, was that Charlemagne's empire should be put back together but by peaceful means – in other words, that the individual nation states must give up their sovereignty and form a United States of Europe. Hitler's attempt to reunite Europe by force did not destroy this European dream. Indeed, the years following his defeat in 1945 gave it a new impetus, especially from the USA, which felt that a United States of Europe would be the best way of containing the menace from the Soviet Union in Western Europe.

At this time, some leading figures in Europe were also advocating a federal superstate as the best way of achieving lasting peace in Europe, claiming that the existence of individual nation states led to wars. This misguided thinking has never caught on elsewhere in the world and wasn't sufficiently widespread among the electorate of any European country for them to be willing democratically to vote away their independence. How, then, could the nations of Europe be persuaded to surrender their sovereignty? – and what would be the means for driving integration forward? The answers came from Jean Monnet, a French Civil Servant, who produced a plan which drew heavily from the considerable volume of material produced by supporters of a federal Europe in the inter-war years. The political project was to be disguised as an economic project. Sovereignty was to be surrendered by little by little - and stealthily - to newly-created European institutions including a Council of Ministers, an assembly, a court and above all, a secretariat. Look up the word "secretariat" in a dictionary and the definition will usually be along the lines of "administrative department." However, Monnet's European secretariat was to be far removed from a pool of typists or humble filing clerks. Its senior staff, whose loyalties were to lie with the new organisation rather than to their own countries, were to be the central source of authority and the engine that would drive European integration. This "secretariat" in due course became the European Commission, led by a team of Commissioners who are hand-picked by the leaders of their countries rather than elected. They are required to take an oath in which they state "I do solemnly undertake: to be completely independent in the performance of my duties, in the general interest of the Communities; in the performance of these duties, neither to seek nor to take instructions from any government or from any other body." As Dan Hannan puts it, the EU blueprint quite deliberately takes supreme power away from the government of the member states and places it instead "in the hands of 'experts'; disinterested technocrats immune to the ballot box."

The first stage in the creation of what is now the EU took place in 1950 when the European Coal and Steel Community (ECSC) was established. Six nations (France, West Germany, Italy, Belgium, Luxembourg and the Netherlands) placed their coal and steel industries under supra-national control. The ECSC evolved into the European Economic Community, established by the Treaty of Rome in 1957 and containing the same six nations. These developments would not have been able possible without the support of politicians from these six countries. In the 1950s, with the Second World War fresh in people's memories, there is no question that this generation of politicians deliberately kept the people of their countries in the dark as to the long-term objective of the EEC, although some of them at least may have done so at least in part out of a genuine desire to prevent another war. Unfortunately, they ended up creating a monster.

The UK had been a bystander in these developments. While European integration had the support of Winston Churchill, he was adamant, as was noted earlier, that our country's role was to facilitate the creation of a United States of Europe but not to be part of it. In 1940, there had been no fewer than 10,000 members of the British Federal Union, but the majority of our countrymen were one with Churchill in wishing to retain our national sovereignty. Neither the Labour nor Conservative parties wanted to commit the UK to joining the ECSC, in spite of American pressure to do so in the period after 1945. It has frequently been claimed that, had we been present at the beginning of the discussions leading up to the setting up of the Common Market, we could have influenced its development so that it would have been less federalist – in other words, it would have been more of an economic and less a political project. This is nonsense. It was never meant to be just a trading bloc. Its objective from the very beginning was to create a superstate. We were frozen out because we wanted to preserve our sovereignty. Harold Macmillan and Edward Heath, two of the first senior UK politicians to embrace the European project knew this full well. However, it was still presented to the UK electorate as an economic project – and in the 1960s the economic arguments were quite persuasive, as the economies of the original six members were flourishing while ours languished. We were well qualified to the title of "the sick man of Europe" years before we joined, with our industries blighted by union militancy and a lack of innovation. We regained our competitiveness in the 1980s, but by then it was too late. We had signed up to domination by a foreign bureaucracy and it has cost us dearly.

Legislation the motor of European Union

It is the European Commission which has the responsibility for proposing new legislation. This legislation is the motor of "ever closer union" - a phrase which originated in the preamble to the Treaty of Rome. This political element is not necessarily apparent in every single piece of legislation, but anyone browsing through EU websites will not have to go far before coming across the word "harmonisation." If the objective is to build a United States of Europe, this is perfectly understandable, but so often it creates inconveniences for member states, particularly the UK. It is not just because of our legal system or more obvious areas like the use of imperial measurements or driving on the left where we find ourselves out of step with most other EU member states. Take water standards for example. There may have been a need for the former Eastern Bloc countries to improve the quality of drinking water, but in our country, it was safe to drink tap water many years before we joined the EU. However, the water industry has been forced by the EU's Water Framework Directive to improve the quality of water far beyond what is necessary for safety. We have had to jettison our own sensible and perfectly adequate legislation to "harmonise" with EU standards.

Some of these standards have a "lowest common denominator"

element. Take the Landfill Directive, for example, which has been responsible for some councils ending their weekly bin collections. This was introduced because Denmark and Holland, two small, fairly flat EU member states, have run out of holes in which to bury rubbish. Rather than leave them to sort out the problem for themselves, the Commission stepped in with legislation which applies to all member states. Regardless of the availability of suitable holes in which to bury waste, all 28 nations must find alternatives to landfill, even if this means smelly, air-polluting incinerators. Our railway industry also suffers from unnecessary legislation. The Interoperability Directive introduced a very complex procedure for the registration of new trains to enable them to operate across international boundaries and all new trains introduced in the UK have to comply, even if the vast majority of trains in our country, for obvious reasons of geography, will not be crossing international boundaries. As if that was not enough, the Commission has decreed that those few that do must have priority over domestic trains on certain designated "freight corridors", even if the international train in question may be a freight train limited to 75mph which shares tracks with 125mph domestic passenger trains, thus potentially slowing them down.

How widespread is the damage caused by EU regulation? There has been much debate about the percentage of laws which now come from the EU. A figure of 70% is often quoted, although the EU-funded European Movement rather implausibly claims that the true figure is under 10%. The Open Europe think tank has devoted much time and effort to obtaining a precise figure, but has concluded that, "it's virtually impossible to determine with any degree of certainty what the share of EU-derived laws is." In many ways, the percentage is irrelevant. Anything above 0% is too high when we consider the underlying objective. We do not need the European Commission to submerge our sovereignty under a weight of legislation. There may well have been only 17,356 laws on the EU database on 1st October 2009 but according to Open Europe, a mere 100 of these regulations are costing the UK £27.4 billion each year.

Harder and harder to say "no"

The Commission may initiate legislation, but it does not have the power to put laws on to the statute books of the member states. This is the job of the Council of Ministers (the government ministers from the member states) and the European Parliament. As with the procedure for creating laws in our own parliament, once the initial Commission document appears, it goes through a consultation period, and the final piece of legislation that is passed may bear little resemblance to the original Commission document, having been amended following scrutiny by the Parliament's committees or the representatives of the member states. Once it is known that a piece of legislation is in the pipeline, perhaps as a result of an article in the press, MEPs will find their e-mail inboxes fill up with requests from constituents, businesses, pressure groups and so on, asking them to support or reject certain amendments to the legislation.

Of course, it is possible to stop proposed EU legislation ever getting on to the statute books. A particularly stupid proposal from the Commission to ban unmarked olive oil jugs from restaurant tables was wisely kicked into the long grass following a public outcry across a number of member states, but all too many equally meddlesome regulations do not get booted out and it has become progressively harder for any member state to prevent unwelcome legislation being passed. The UK government fought a long battle with the European Commission over the use of red diesel by the leisure boating industry. Traditionally, pleasure craft have been able to use this fuel, which used to be subject to a much lower level of duty than ordinary diesel. Not content with insisting that as from 2008 a higher rate of duty must be paid, the Commission threatened to fine boat users from the UK if they stray outside UK waters with red diesel in their tanks. The European Commission doesn't seem to care about the contempt in which it is held, even though it fans the flames of euroscepticism across the Continent. It carries on with its proposals to create Europe-wide standards in areas which, to any normal person, would be regarded as most unimportant and trivial. In November 2013 a proposal emerged to standardise lavatory flushing across the 28 member states!

Why do we put up with this interference in our country's affairs? The answer is simple: our political leaders granted the right for the EU to interfere by the signing of various treaties which surrendered areas of national sovereignty. After the Treaty of Rome in 1957, no further treaties were signed until 1986, when the Single European Act was passed. This was followed by the treaties of Maastricht (1992), Amsterdam (1997), Nice (2001) and Lisbon (2010). Every one of these treaties, especially Maastricht and Lisbon, saw the member states voluntarily giving up more power. Power was surrendered by two methods:-

- An increase in the number of EU "competences" – in other words, the areas of government which are the responsibility of the EU, either in entirety (exclusive competences, where only the EU can legislate and adopt legally binding acts) or in part (shared competences, where either the EU or a member state can legislate, although the EU is very much the senior partner, allowing the member state to legislate only where the EU chooses not to do so). Areas of exclusive competence now include trade, competition rules and marine conservation, while agriculture, social policy, transport, energy supply and environmental issues are among the shared competences.
- A surrender of national vetoes. Fewer and fewer decisions in the areas of EU responsibility are now decided by unanimity, with most now decided by Qualified Majority Voting – a system whereby the representative of each member state in a meeting of the Council of Ministers has a vote weighted roughly according to the population of their country. Thus the UK counts for 29 votes whereas Malta is worth only 3. It does mean that the UK's vote currently counts only 8.3% of the total and even though the rather complex rules require a greater majority than 50% of all votes cast, we can easily be outvoted. We can ask the other member states for an exemption, or derogation, from all or part of the legislation. Alternatively, a member state can be allowed to defer

implementation of legislation to allow time for an industry to adjust that may suffer particularly from the effects of the legislation. However, if the other member states don't agree and we're outvoted, then we've got no choice but to obey. No country has ever refused to put EU legislation that has been signed off at European level on to its statute books. Further national vetoes will be lost on 1st November 2014 when the new areas of qualified majority voting agreed in Lisbon Treaty come into force.

It is only when an individual, industry or interest group comes up against the damaging effect of EU legislation that it becomes apparent just how much power has already been surrendered. In November 2011, Sir Mervyn King, the former governor of the Bank of England, lost his temper and directed some pretty strong language to the European Union's internal markets Commissioner Michel Barnier, who threatened to interfere in the running of Britain's banks. Unfortunately, thanks to Gordon Brown's signing of the Lisbon Treaty, which surrendered a further 63 national vetoes to the EU, Barnier had gained a legal right so to do, a fact of which Sir Mervyn was hitherto unaware. The leisure boat industry, mentioned above, did persuade both MEPs and their national representatives to lobby for the UK to be allowed to continue to fill up their boats with red diesel at the lower rate of duty, but for all their efforts, the derogation (exemption) was not renewed after 2008, and all our elected representatives could do was to say sorry. They were powerless. It is hardly surprising that neither politicians nor much of the mainstream media are keen for the public to know just how much of our day-to-day lives are affected by decisions now made in Brussels. Rather than admitting their powerlessness, their usual tactic is to focus on some trivial concession they were able to extract. No fewer than 55 attempts by our ministers in the last 20 years to block EU legislation have failed, but our government doesn't want us to know just how little influence we really have. Not only is this dishonest, but it poses the question as to how much it really cares.

Far worse than the problems of the leisure boating industry is the

EU's ban on testing certain potentially life-saving cancer drugs on children, Professor Alan Ashworth, head of the UK's Institute of Cancer Research, claims that EU regulation is causing unnecessary suffering and even death, among children suffering from cancer: "Modern cancer treatments are often targeted at genetic features of the tumour that may be common to a number of tumour types, and to adults' and children's cancers. That means a drug developed for a cancer in adults could also be effective against a cancer affecting a completely different part of the body in children. The way EU rules are implemented fails to take this into account," he said.

Dynamite the Berlaymont!

We will return to the costs of all these regulations in more detail in Chapter 5. Unsurprisingly, it is not just the UK which is complaining about how business is hampered by EU regulation. Even José Manuel Barroso, outgoing President of the European Commission, has admitted that EU regulation should be more business friendly, but this is not the point. David Cameron might possibly persuade the present European Commission to make regulation less onerous, but if a future Commission reverses direction and adds to the burden of regulation, there is little any future British Prime Minister can do as long as we are members of the EU. David Cameron and William Hague pledged to bring to an end the fundamental EU doctrine of "Ever Closer Union." It is hard to believe they will be able to break the stranglehold of the European Commission. It was designed to be the motor of European integration and still manifestly fulfils that very same purpose all these years later. As long as it is in existence, it will remain a threat to our national prosperity, sovereignty and liberty. Only if its vast headquarters in the hideously ugly Berlaymont Building in Brussels is blown up, the 28 Commissioners and their staff given their marching orders and the UK's relationship with the rest of the EU confined solely to trade issues should Cameron and Hague's claim be taken seriously. This is really asking for the moon for, while UK business moans about the European Commission, a yet grander role is being sought for it elsewhere in the EU. Take, for instance, Pascal

Lamy, an influential French Socialist, disciple of the infamous Jacques Delors and former Director General of the World Trade Organisation. He has proposed the direct election of Commissioners, but in return, the Commission would gain greater power still."I refuse to countenance this...idea that the Commission is merely the secretariat of an executive council," he wrote. His plan would reduce the role of the European Council, which is the forum for representatives from the Member states' governments, while allowing the Commission greater power to drive the Federalist agenda forward by such measures as the raising of taxes at EU level, rather than the member states sending contributions to Brussels. A frightening scenario indeed, but of even greater significance was the recent statement by Angela Merkel, the German Chancellor, that "The European Commission will one day become a government, the European Council a second chamber and the European Parliament will have more powers."

Given such high-level support for increasing, rather than decreasing the power of the European Commission, it is therefore most likely that the Commission building will still be standing and functioning when any referendum takes place. If so, no one who cares about their country should vote to remain within the EU. We cannot allow unelected foreign bureaucrats to wreak any further damage on our country. They have already done more than enough.

Chapter 4
It would open the way for better politicians

The message from the three previous chapters is not just that we have surrendered our power of self-government, lost many of our ancient liberties and are drowning under a flood of regulation produced by an institution committed to building a federal superstate, but also that **our political leadership has been complicit in the process.** It is appalling that from 1st January 2015, MPs will earn £74,000 per year plus expenses when much of their work has been sub-contracted to Brussels. In 1972, the last year in which MPs actually did 100% of the job we pay them to do, their salary was only £4,500, barely 6% of their current rate of remuneration. We could begin the process of regaining our freedom tomorrow if we were led by decent politicians. The following chapters of this book include quotes from a number of eminent economists who have produced detailed studies proving that leaving the EU would not lead to economic calamity, but none of this evidence has so far caused any shift of opinion among the leaders of Britain's three biggest political parties, nor among their friends in the BBC, the Foreign Office or the leaders of big business such as Richard Branson. And nor is it likely to. It is impossible to imagine any of these people, who between them wield a considerable degree of power, having a "Damascus Road" experience between now and any future vote on leaving the EU. Indeed, David Cameron has been quite explicit that he wants Britain to remain a member of the EU and when asked by the Spanish *El Pais* newspaper in April 2013 whether he would withdraw the UK from the EU in the event of an "out" vote, his reply, translated back into

English, comes out as something like "I don't like it." There will be much foot-dragging by whoever is Prime Minister before the will of the people is obeyed. Unfortunately, 40 years of EEC/EU membership has adversely affected our politicians. Like their counterparts in Brussels, they prefer stability to democracy, hence the reason why a "no" vote would be so uncomfortable for them. So, to put it another way, a successful UK withdrawal will have been like a Norman Wisdom film - a classic struggle where the heroic underdogs - the ordinary British people - finally and against the odds come out on top of their powerful opponents.

Distorting the facts

The way our political class has hidden the truth about the EU in recent decades is nothing less than disgraceful. We were taken into the EEC under false pretences in 1973 and this has set an appalling precedent. Politicians have often tried to undermine their opponents by scaremongering. The "three million jobs" myth, to which we will refer again in Chapter 7, is one of the worst examples of this, being based on a blatant distortion of facts. The figure of three million jobs, or more exactly, 3.2 million jobs, which were linked to our membership of the EU, first appeared in a report produced by Dr. Martin Weale in 2000 for the National Institute for Economic and Social Research. However, the report actually said:-

Detailed estimates from input-output tables suggest that up to 3.2 million UK jobs are now associated directly with exports of goods and services to other EU countries. This has given rise to popular concern that some of these jobs might be at risk if Britain were to leave the Union. Opponents of membership on the other hand argue that many of the benefits flowing from the increasingly integrated European Economic Area might still be available even if the UK were to withdraw, particularly since the Uruguay Round Agreement has imposed significant limits on the trade barriers that the EU can place on non-members. In conjunction with the potential gains from withdrawing from the Common Agricultural Policy and no longer paying net fiscal contributions to the EU, there is a case that withdrawal from the EU might actually offer our nation net economic benefits.

The report did **not** say that these jobs would be lost if we left the EU. Far from it. It suggested that withdrawal may actually be beneficial. It was the Britain in Europe cross-party group, which campaigned unsuccessfully for Britain to join the euro and which included such figures as Ken Clarke, Tony Blair, Michael Heseltine and Charles Kennedy, who started the scaremongering. Unsurprisingly, Dr. Weale was furious at this distortion of the findings of his research, describing it as "pure Goebbels" (a reference to Hitler's Minister of Propaganda) and saying, "in many years of academic research I cannot recall such a wilful distortion of the facts". However, the distortion has been repeated over and over again, perhaps in the hope that if the lie is repeated enough it will become accepted as truth. Nick Clegg regurgitated it in January 2013 in the wake of David Cameron's announcement of a referendum on our membership of the EU and John Prescott followed suit four months later. Danny Alexander, the Treasury minister, (and surprise, surprise, another Liberal Democrat) recycled this rubbish to an audience in Washington as recently as June 2014. Will some people never give up?

Even worse was the lie told by Peter Hain, the Europe minister under the last Labour government. When after 18 months' work, the draft EU Constitution first appeared, Valéry Giscard d'Estaing, the former French President and chairman of the group which produced it, was most excited, comparing the project to the gathering in Philadelphia in 1787 which produced the American constitution. "We will have a structure in which we will have federalistic functions… We will have a sort of government in the making," he said. However, Peter Hain, the Europe Minister in the Labour government at the time, dismissed the project as merely a "tidying-up exercise" for if the true nature of the project which surrendered over 60 national vetoes, was let out of the bag, demands for a UK referendum would have been hard to resist.

Vested Interest

Another badly-behaved group of the europhile political class is the Business for New Europe campaign group, which is leading the fight against withdrawal. Its website claims that its leaders are "a coalition of business leaders" who "support Britain's membership of the EU." A glance at the profiles of the leading figures tells a different story. Sir Leon Brittan was a former European Commissioner, and Lord Kerr and Sir Nigel Steinwald are career diplomats who have headed the UK's permanent representation to the EU. Men like this are often offered company directorships on their retirement, but does this turn them into bona fide businessmen entitled to speak for the entire business community? Hardly. The group's chairman, Roland Rudd, was closely involved with Tony Blair and Peter Mandelson in their re-branding of the Labour party. He could be called a businessman of sorts, but his "business" turns out to be a lobbying firm, RLM Finsbury. You won't find the word "lobbying" on the company's website, but it does mention "integrated political and media campaigns", which is another way of saying the same thing. It is no surprise that those who do very nicely working on behalf of clients (usually big business) to represent their interests in the corridors of Brussels are none too keen to see this lucrative source of income curtailed. Many large businesses have done well out of the UK's membership of the EU. They support EU regulation and are keen to influence its direction, because once they have complied with it, the regulation helps protect them from smaller and newer competitors who haven't. There is no need to talk of conspiracy theory here. It is a coalition of self-interest. In the words of Rev. Dr Peter Mullen, a caustic critic of Britain's membership of the EU, "people in power will naturally base their policy decisions on those things which are most likely to have good consequences for themselves." They don't care about ordinary people and certainly have no appreciation of our great history as a self-governing nation. Rudd was previously involved in the pro-Euro Britain in Europe pressure group. Given the ongoing crisis in the Eurozone, the statements put out by this group now seem laughable. For instance, in 2002, Charles Kennedy said,

"The Euro, despite the gloomy predictions from anti-Europeans, has proved to be a success. We cannot afford to be isolated from our biggest and closest trading partner any longer." Likewise the apocalyptic warnings of Business for New Europe must be taken with a pinch of salt.

For today's career politicians, especially those whose working life began as a research assistants to an MP and who thus have never held down a job outside of politics, the EU provides a well-paid safety net for anyone whose domestic political career takes a tumble. When I began my spell working as a researcher in the European Parliament in 2006, several "ghosts of British politics past" could be found among the MEPs, including Phillip Whitehead, a former Labour MP who lost his Derbyshire seat in 1983, and Baroness Emma Nicholson, a Tory MP who defected to the Liberal Democrats. Of course, some really spectacular political failures, such as Neil Kinnock and Peter Mandelson, have done even better, ending up as European Commissioners, commanding six-figure salaries without having to win any election to reach their exalted position. (As was noted in Chapter 3, commissioners are appointed, rather than chosen by ballot.) Given the pampered lifestyle on offer, with generous expenses, it is no surprise that former MPs who began their careers favouring withdrawal from the EU subsequently change their minds on relocating to Brussels and "go native". It now seems incredible to believe that on 8th January 1986, Neil Kinnock said, "We believe there should be reforms in the EEC which would benefit all the members. If these were not achieved, our policy is to preserve the ultimate option of withdrawing Britain."

The civil servants of the Foreign Office also have a vested interest in supporting our membership of the European Union. Sir Simon Fraser, the current senior policy advisor to the Foreign Secretary and head of the Diplomatic Service, previously served two spells as chief of staff to Britain's European Commissioners, with a further spell in the Foreign Office in between. He is a typical example of the career civil servant who has made a successful career by switching from Whitehall to Brussels and back. Indeed, even before 1991, when the

Foreign Office started a scheme for "high fliers" which prepared them for working with Brussels, this department was stuffed full of europhiles. It certainly was in 1986, when Margaret Thatcher signed the Single European Act, which surrendered a significant number of national powers to Brussels. She later admitted her mistake, but it was too late. She had been deliberately misled by civil servants in the Foreign Office who convinced her that the Single European Act was primarily about reducing trade barriers. Anyone committed to the sovereignty of the nation state, if they are able to get into the Foreign Office in the first place, would clearly find their career prospects severely limited. Brussels (and the UN in New York too, for that matter) would be closed to them, as they would be totally out of place among ardent believers in the authority of top-down trans-national institutions that dominate the political landscape in these places. When Ian Mansfield, a civil servant in the Foreign Office, won the Institute of Economic Affairs' €100,000 prize for the best essay on how our country could leave the EU, he was banned for a while from giving interviews. Even though he stressed that the work was his own and did not represent the views of the Foreign Office, his triumph was clearly an embarrassment to his employer.

No sacking for surrender

UK ministers cannot be relied upon to put their country or their fellow MPs' interests and concerns first when they represent their country in the Council of Ministers. It is not that some of them try but fail to block legislation; sometimes they do not even try. One dreadful but sadly typical incident took place on 21st June 2013 when Anna Soubry, the Health Minister, was summoned to a meeting of European health ministers in order to secure Europe-wide agreement on its latest legislative proposal – the Tobacco Products Directive which, when transposed into law, will place draconian restrictions on the rights of smokers. Anxious to avoid any delay, Soubry asked the House of Commons' European Scrutiny Committee to waive its right to scrutinise the legislation so she could negotiate the UK's position without hindrance.

The Committee, chaired by Conservative MP Bill Cash, denied her request on the grounds that two weeks was insufficient time to examine the proposed legislation. She ignored their decision, went to Luxembourg, and committed the UK to implementing this wide-ranging legislation even though, according to Soubry's evidence to the Committee, her fellow health ministers didn't even take a vote. Whatever one's opinions of smoking, bypassing the democratically-elected Parliament of the United Kingdom is appalling. Soubry is a supporter of UK membership of the EU but, like her party leader, claims to seek "radical reform." You would think she would have been sacked from her ministerial position for such an abject surrender to a foreign power. However, she remained in her post with no report of her being given even a modest dressing-down, even though it is inconceivable that the Prime Minister was unaware of her actions. This underscores the point about the complicity of the UK government made earlier in the chapter. Ken Clarke, the europhile Tory MP recently provided further confirmation: "The idea that heroic British ministers sit here trying to stem the flow {of EU rules} is a myth," he said. "It is very hard to find an EU regulation that has been forced on an unwilling British minister who voted against it." He added that he could not think of one EU regulation passed into UK law that had not been first advocated by a British minister or official. So here we have it straight from the horse's mouth. Our senior politicians, whether Labour, LibDem or Tory, do not want us to know just how many day-to-day issues are now controlled by the EU and when it emerges that some unpopular piece of legislation originates with the EU, they are happy for the public to vent their anger on Brussels in order to draw attention away from their own culpability in this appalling process.

If further evidence were needed of the complicity of most of our leading politicians in the betrayal of our country, we could do worse than consider how the EU (Approvals) Bill was handled in the House of Commons. This Bill, which received its second reading in January 2014, covered a number of EU-related issues, but most of the debate centred on the Europe Citizens' Programme, a five-year programme costing €185 billion to fund educational projects that seek to enhance both the understanding of EU institutions and "European integration". In other words, as one MP put it: "this grant-making exercise is aimed at providing propaganda, as I see it, for purposes of political union." Only 32 MPs opposed it at this second reading, and just a couple of weeks later it went through its final stages with only 30 MPs opposing. We, the UK taxpayers, have been committed by our democratically-elected representatives, to contributing £18 million to a scheme which will allow the EU to infect our schoolchildren with its odious propaganda. You do not need a multi-million pound budget to tell people something is good unless it isn't that good at all. For instance, it did not require millions to be spent telling people that the internet was a good thing. It soon became self-evident. Jacob Rees-Mogg, one of the 32 MPs who opposed the bill, pointed out the contradiction between the purposes of this Bill and the David Cameron's stated intentions: "The Prime Minister said he was against ever closer union; the money that we are discussing will be spent on promoting ever closer union...Can we have trust in our politicians in this nation if the Prime Minister says one thing and his ministers bring forth bills saying another?"

In spite of such damning evidence of two-faced behaviour, no one could deny that there are also a few advocates of Britain's continuing membership of the EU who are honourable and sincere men, albeit misguided. Unfortunately, they are in a minority. The loudest voices clamouring for the UK to remain within the EU are untrustworthy, as we have seen. To suffer defeat in a referendum would therefore be a huge blow for such people, as it means they would have been exposed - in the media, in public debates and in publications like this - as self-serving, peddlers of inaccuracy, duplicitous and wilfully obstinate in the face of overwhelming evidence. Their stock will fall even lower than it currently is, while the leaders of the withdrawalist cause will gain considerable prestige.

At this point, in the interest of fairness it has to be said, sadly, that not every withdrawalist is necessarily a saint or a hero. Some UKIP MEPs, for instance, have been found to have been engaged in less-than-angelic behaviour, but most of the leaders in the battle for UK withdrawal have a positive vision for our country, seeking to reduce bureaucracy, increase political accountability and freedom and to restore our national prosperity and liberty. In the main, they are predominantly people who do not believe that politicians, whether in Westminster or Brussels, should be micro-managing the lives of ordinary men, women and children Their numbers include economists, businessmen, think tanks and a number of members of the Houses of Parliament. Sadly, MPs with longstanding withdrawalist credentials don't tend to rise up the ministerial ladder. Certainly, until last year, any Conservative MP aspiring to even a junior ministerial position would have found their hopes dashed if their support for withdrawal was made public. David Cameron has been determined to keep such men on the back benches. Sadly, he would rather tolerate the pathetic surrender typified by Anna Soubry (see above) than allow a determined supporter of UK independence to rise to ministerial level and fight our country's corner in the meetings of the Council of Ministers with the same panache as Nigel Farage and Daniel Hannan display in the European Parliament. Nevertheless, recent statements expressing support for withdrawal made by some of his Cabinet ministers, including Iain Duncan-Smith and Michael Gove, are to be welcomed, Support for withdrawal in the Labour Party is more limited, but Austin Mitchell MP and John Mills, a significant Labour Party donor, share the same commitment to accountable government as their Conservative withdrawalist colleagues. The Labour Euro-Safeguards Campaign, of which they are prominent leaders, expresses concern on its website at "the patent lack of democracy within the EU, leaving far too much power with unelected and unaccountable bureaucrats, bankers and judges."

These are the men and women whose public standing will receive a boost from withdrawal. They will not put their feet up and say "job done" if the UK votes to leave. Firstly, they will put considerable pressure on the Prime Minister, whoever he might be, to obey the will of the people, and secondly, they must not and surely will not let matters rest when we leave the EU but rather will use the opportunity to address the deceit, cronyism, unaccountability and "know-it-all" attitudes that have so poisoned British politics since our accession to the EEC/EU in 1973. Political life in our country needs a good shake-up; a recent opinion poll suggested that only 1 in 12 of those surveyed believed that MPs put the interest of their constituents first, and only 6% believed that they put their country first. This chapter has shown that such a negative view of our elected representatives is fully justified. Withdrawal from the EU will certainly create an upheaval in Westminster. One can but hope that politics in this country will be greatly improved as a result.

Chapter 5
We should benefit financially

The political arguments in favour of withdrawal are overwhelming, as has been shown in the first four chapters, but what of the financial arguments? Can we afford to withdraw? Does independence carry so high an economic price that we must grin and bear it and remain in the EU, watching our independence ebb away, in order to avoid Armageddon? This is the message given out by some supporters of our EU membership. Our only realistic choice, we are told, is to embark on "a gruelling struggle to retain influence in a club that increasingly revolves around the Eurozone." They claim withdrawal would be "the road to economic ruin," "calamitous" and a move which would result in "great damage to business." However, if this were so, why has not any UK government, with help from Brussels, produced a definitive cost/benefit analysis to prove the point? Instead, we have been fobbed off with the flawed "Balance of Competences" reviews and vacuous platitudes such as a statement on the website of the UK office of the European Commission stating that "it is far too simplistic and perverse to confine the European Union to a price tag." This condescending attitude goes back to the days of the accession talks. Dr Eric Edmond, a civil servant at that time who subsequently worked in the Bank of England, mentioned to his colleagues in an informal conversation that he would like to see the cost benefit analysis of joining the then Common Market. He was told not to ask silly questions as it was perfectly obvious to everyone that there was huge benefit to the UK from joining!

It has been left to non-governmental organisations to analyse the costs of UK membership. Their evidence suggests that immediately upon independence, things might be a bit turbulent for certain sectors of the economy if withdrawal did not go smoothly, but the long-term economic prospects look very positive. Within five years of withdrawal, everyone would be looking back and wondering what all the fuss had been about.

One of the earliest independent studies of the consequences of leaving the EU was undertaken in 1996 for the Institute of Economic Affairs. It suggested that the net effect of withdrawal would be negligible and if the right trading arrangements were in place after withdrawal, a modest saving would result. Two studies published in 2000 came to contradictory conclusions. The Institute of Directors calculated that we should be better off out, whereas the National Institute of Economic and Social Research came to the opposite conclusion. A decade or so later, the subsequent deluge of EU regulation appears to have tipped the balance further in favour of withdrawal. Tim Congdon's *How much does the European Union cost Britain?* estimated that the total cost of EU membership for the average household was £6,000 per year, while Patrick Minford's *Setting business free: into the global economy* places the costs even higher. While other recent studies have not painted such a positive picture, if all the various projections of the economic benefits (or lack of them) from withdrawal were to be aggregated and averaged, the net result would be that we should be better off out. Only the CBI's recent report *Our global future* is currently suggesting that EU membership had brought overall economic benefits and its methodology was subject to widespread criticism, even from the pro-EU Open Europe think tank. However, John Cridland, the CBI's Director General, has at least distanced himself from the most apocalyptic scare stories. "The UK could survive outside the EU" he said and David Cameron has also admitted that Britain would not collapse if it left. Ian Mansfield, winner of the prize sponsored by the Institute of Economic Affairs for the best essay on how to withdraw from the EU, suggested that a best-case scenario would see us 1.1% better off and the most likely outcome being growth of 0.1%. However, Dr Richard North, who also submitted an entry for this competition, would not be drawn on any sort of figure. He argues that withdrawal would "deliver beneficial effects, but the uncertainty renders any estimates of future trade and other matters impossible to quantify accurately."

There are many reasons why it is impossible to ascertain exactly how much better off the UK would become on independence. A short book like this can only touch on a few issues. For example, the cost of implementing literally thousands of EU regulations is impossible to work out in any sort of detail, Furthermore, as has been noted, much depends on the relationship we negotiate with the EU on exit. However, some savings can be identified and calculated with a reasonable degree of accuracy.

The direct costs

When Edward Heath negotiated the terms of UK membership, it was agreed right from the start that we would be a net contributor to the European budget - in other words, we would pay out more than we would receive back. Heath had to agree to these grovelling terms to appease the French. General de Gaulle, the French President, had twice vetoed our membership, as he did not believe that we would be willing to support the Common Agricultural Policy, which was, and indeed still is, a subsidy for French farmers.

Direct contributions include VAT revenue, sugar levies, customs receipts and a so-called Gross National Income payment. In total, they appear relatively small. According the *Pink Book* (HM Treasury's annual statistics on the UK budget), we paid £9.3 billion in 2011 and £10.5 billion in 2012. The 2012 figure works out at only just over £160 per person, or £640 for a family of four. This may seem a tiny amount, but how many hard-pressed UK families would rather have an extra £640 per year (or roughly £12 per week) to help pay their food and energy bills rather than giving it to the EU? Alternatively, scrapping our direct payments would enable the government to abolish Insurance Premium Tax, Landfill tax and Inheritance Tax while still having extra funds available to pay off some of the budget deficit.

To confuse matters, another Government document, *HM Treasury European Union Finances 2012*, comes up with a different figure, giving a gross contribution of over £15 million or 2010 and 2011, with similar estimates for 2012 and 2013. As Tim Congdon explains, the difference is caused by the first set of figures relating to payments by the UK government to the EU, while the other includes all payments made to the EU, including those by non-government bodies. Of course, the net figures, which deduct the money we receive back, are lower, but how much do we gain from EU largesse? Unless you are either a farmer or involved in a project such as the reopening of the Welsh Highland Railway from Caernarfon to Porthmadog, which received over £5.7 million in EU funding, you do not benefit at all. Some of the money returned to the UK is basically nothing more than bribery to support the EU. It is hardly surprising that you don't hear much criticism of the EU from Friends of the Earth. In 2011, Friends of the Earth Europe received nearly €1.2 million in funds from EU sources – nearly 46% of its total annual budget.

These direct costs are only going to get higher. Margaret Thatcher negotiated a deal in 1984 at Fontainebleau in France which reduced our payment, as she felt that the method used to calculate it was unfair, Unfortunately, Tony Blair agreed in 2005 to give up much of the rebate over a period of time, on the grounds that the countries from Eastern Europe which had recently joined the EU needed financial assistance, so we must "transfer wealth from rich countries to poor countries", and that we were, "investing in Eastern Europe." The British people are remarkably generous in supporting worthy causes, voluntarily giving millions of pounds in relief aid following last year's typhoon in the Philippines, for instance, but we have no choice about this international compulsory wealth redistribution. We were never consulted as to whether we wanted to support the worthy cause of improving the infrastructure of Eastern Europe. It was certainly not included in Labour's 2005 election manifesto. The more poor countries join the EU in the future - and there are several in the queue - the more we shall have to cough up.

The costs of regulation

EU regulation, as we saw in Chapter 3, is the motor of European integration. It also carries a considerable financial cost. Even businesses wishing to see the UK remain within the EU acknowledge that regulation is burdensome. Lord Leach, Chairman of Open Europe, says that businesses worry about the "dampening effect of Brussels regulation on firms competing in global markets." David Cameron's earlier talk of renegotiating the terms of UK membership is now seemingly to be pursued alongside an EU-wide attempt to cut back on regulation, which has won the support of Germany and the Netherlands. However, even the proposed "Red Cards," first proposed by David Lidington, the Europe Minister, which would allow a majority of national parliaments to block unwanted EU laws do not go far enough, for they would not address the problem caused by the mountain of existing legislation. Nor does the "one in, one out" proposal of the UK Government's Business Taskforce, which would insist on one piece of legislation being jettisoned for every new proposal. At the very minimum, national parliaments need to be given the power unilaterally to ditch regulations that are felt to be unhelpful while the European Commission (which is the source of these regulations) should be abolished. We know that these ideas will not be on the table if David Cameron begins any negotiations, for this was more or less the main proposal of the letter written in January 2014 by Bernard Jenkin and signed by a further 94 of his fellow Tory MPs. William Hague, the Foreign Secretary at the time, called the idea "unrealistic" and sadly, with good reason. The principle of the irreversibility of the so-called acquis communautaire – the policy areas which national governments have surrendered to the European Union - will remain sacrosanct. The European Parliament and other heads of state are unlikely to agree any change to the principle that no powers once surrendered can be regained. It makes no difference whether David Cameron tries to reform the whole EU or renegotiate the terms of the UK's membership. His party claims to have sought reform for many years. Juncker's appointment has exposed the futility of this agenda. **A few minor powers at the most may be**

repatriated; a few pieces of legislation may be jettisoned, the pace of integration may be slowed, but the necessary change of direction will not happen. The Dutch government, which also claims to support EU reform, isn't keen on treaty changes. This is partly, no doubt, out of concern that any referendum would result in a "no" vote. However, its attitude further underlines the point that will be no significant repatriation of powers already surrendered under the existing treaties. We can never have any confidence in a permanent reduction of the damage caused by EU legislation unless we leave the EU, for any reforms which Cameron and his allies may achieve could easily be reversed by a future Commission, or by a majority of the other member states.

Various estimates have been made of the current cost of EU regulation. Tim Congdon puts it at 5-6% of Gross Domestic Product (GDP - the total value of goods and services produced by a country), or about £80 billion per year. Patrick Minford reckons it is even more costly – suggesting it may even account for as much as 25% of GDP. Even pro-EU sources have acknowledged the damaging cost of legislation. In October 2006, Gunther Verheugen, the European Commissioner for industry and enterprise estimated that the annual cost of EU regulation across the EU was 5.5% of GDP, while Peter Mandelson told the Confederation of British Industry as far back as 2004 that while the supposed benefits of EU membership amounted to 1.5% of GDP, the cost of regulation amounted to 4%.

For all the variation in these estimates, there is a consensus that EU regulation costs us more than our direct contributions. One of the most detailed analyses so far has been Open Europe's list of the most costly EU directives, which was published in December 2009. This research claims that the worst 100 will cumulatively cost the UK a staggering £184 billion by 2020 unless we regain our independence. At the top of the list is the Working Time Directive 93/104/EC, which limits the number of hours an employee may work per week. This single directive costs the UK economy £3.5 billion per annum, or over £230 for every family of four. One example of how it adversely affects us came to light in 2012, when it was revealed that in 2011 and 2012 it cost the NHS £1 billion per year employing temporary staff - including at least one doctor who was paid £20,000 per week - because their full-time colleagues may not work more than 48 hours per week. Other particularly costly directives are the Climate Change and Renewable Energy package and the Buildings and Approved Inspectors (amendment) Regulations of 2006 (Articles 3-6 of Directive 2002/91/EC), which cost the UK economy an estimated £3 billion and £2.2 billion per annum respectively.

The Lisbon Treaty handed control of financial regulation to the EU, and since the Open Europe list was published, some 20 directives in areas relating to bank capital, transaction taxes and market infrastructure have been proposed, which threaten the prosperity of the City of London. Indeed, with London being the leading financial centre in Europe, these regulations will affect our capital city more than anywhere else in Europe, yet they were devised by politicians who have no love for this country. "It is our deliberate intention to damage the City, We want something of what you have got," said one EU official to the eurosceptic Lord Howard Flight recently. The French in particular are very jealous that most currency transactions involving the Euro take place in the UK – i.e., outside the Eurozone. The fact that most currency transactions involving the Saudi Arabian Riyal also take place in the City does not cause similar resentment in Riyadh.

There are thousands of EU-inspired laws which have been transposed on to the UK statute books and, as it would take some time to review them all and decide which are actually sensible (and therefore worth keeping), we would not reap the financial benefit immediately on our withdrawal from the EU. However, the worst culprits, like those mentioned above, have already been identified and given that it will take a while for an "out" vote to translate into actual withdrawal, there ought to be sufficient time in the transition period to prepare the ground for repealing these laws on the very day we regain our independence.

And a few more costs

It would also take a while for an independent UK to benefit from the end of what Tim Congdon calls the "costs of resource misallocation" – in other words, where our membership of the EU impairs our efficiency. The most infamous resource misallocation is the Common Agricultural Policy (CAP), which is a subsidy to our competitors – foreign farmers. The CAP was devised when memories of food shortages resulting from World War 2 were still fresh in people's minds. Self-sufficiency in food was viewed as an objective to be pursued at almost any price. French farmers in particular received subsidies to produce food regardless of how inefficient their farming practices were. When they produced too much food, it was either exported at extremely low prices to Third World countries, undercutting the prices paid to local farmers, or else left to rot. After this era of "butter mountains" and "wine lakes", the principle of "setaside" was introduced, where farmers were paid for doing nothing - leaving fields uncultivated. Meanwhile, subsidies were paid to produce crops that would otherwise have been uneconomical. Tobacco cultivation, for instance, was encouraged, and farmers were paid to produce a variety for which there was very little market.

Further protection for Europe's farmers is provided through import tariffs, making some food from outside the EU more expensive. For example, Kenyan beans, popular in our supermarkets in the winter months when no fresh home-grown produce is available, are subject to a minimum tariff of 13.1%. Reform of the CAP has been a repeated demand of British agricultural ministers over the years, but the intransigence of the French always prevails. The consequences for the UK taxpayer are twofold. Firstly, we are paying £40 billion per year to subsidise European farmers whose methods are far less efficient than those of the small but well-run UK farming sector. Secondly, because we are required to charge import duties on food imported from outside the EU, we cannot buy food as cheaply as we could outside the EU. New Zealand's farmers receive no subsidies and therefore produce food at lower prices than their European counterparts. However, as will be considered in more detail in the chapter on trade, as long as we remain in the EU, we cannot strike a bilateral free trade agreement with this Commonwealth nation.

The British housewife would notice a significant reduction of the cost of her weekly shopping trip if we left the EU. The Organisation of Economic Cooperation and Development estimated as far back as 1993 that the CAP was adding £1,000 per year, or £20 per week, to the average family's food bill. Food prices have risen significantly since then. Kristian Niemietz from the Institute of Economic Affairs states that European food prices in 2005-10 were 11% above world market levels, which is a particular burden on the poorest in society.

Our farmers could not cope with an immediate end to all subsidies immediately we leave the EU and would need some support over the transitional period, but even so, as soon as trade agreements could be struck with food producers outside the EU, food prices would fall.

The examples cited in this chapter are only a small fraction of the financial costs imposed on Britain by the EU. Subsequent chapters will touch on other extra costs, including higher energy bills and job losses. However, before we move on, mention should be made of the many other ways in which our hard-earned cash disappears into the Brussels black hole. Fraud is one particularly notorious example. The EU accounts have not been signed off since 1993. The 2010 report of the European Court of Auditors concluded that "The policy groups Agriculture and Natural Resources and Cohesion, Energy and Transport are materially affected by error. The Court's estimate for the most likely error rate for payments underlying the accounts is 3.7%. In the Court's opinion, because of the significance of the matters described on the legality and regularity of payments underlying the accounts paragraph, the payments underlying the accounts for the year ended 31 December 2010 are materially affected by error." A recent report produced by Cecilia Malmström, the EU's Home Affairs Commissioner, claimed that fraud costs the EU €120 billion (£99 billion) each year, a figure she described as "breathtaking."

Would withdrawal increase costs anywhere?

It is only fair to point out that a few extra costs would be incurred if we left the EU. Like most of the costs mentioned in this chapter, they cannot be quantified exactly, as it depends on the post-withdrawal scenario. We may find that some home-grown foodstuffs such as fruit become more expensive if the pool of cheap Eastern European labour dries up. The willingness of these workers to put in very long hours for low wages has boosted agricultural productivity and has unquestionably helped keep food prices down.

Less prosperous areas which have benefited from regional funding through the European Regional Development Fund and the European Social Fund may also feel that withdrawal carries a cost. On 2nd November 2012, Leanne Wood, the leader of Plaid Cymru, launched a strong attack on Labour during BBC's Any Questions programme because the party joined forces with Tory rebels to call for a real-term cut in EU spending between 2014 and 2020 and thus defeat the government, which merely wanted a freeze. She claimed that this would mean less regional aid for Wales. Maybe she is right, but it is an appalling humiliation for any part of a once-great nation like the UK to be reduced to taking a begging bowl to a foreign power. Anyway, the amount we receive back from the EU is much smaller than our direct contribution.

The debate about the cost of our EU membership is likely to run and run until we leave. This chapter has only provided the briefest of summaries, but has nonetheless provided sufficient evidence to show that our membership of the EU has not been good value for money - and not just for the UK. A recent study by the consultancy group Capital Economics for the Dutch PVV party suggested that if the Netherlands left the EU, Dutch GDP would increase by 10-13% by 2035.

If yet more confirmation is needed, it can be provided by considering just how much better off the EU's two most significant non-members have become.

Support from overseas

Unlike our government, the Swiss government did conduct a cost/benefit analysis of replacing its series of bilateral agreements with the EU with full membership, and concluded that EU membership would cost more than **six times** its present arrangement of bilateral treaties. The benefits to Norway of remaining outside the European Union can best be illustrated from the graph below.

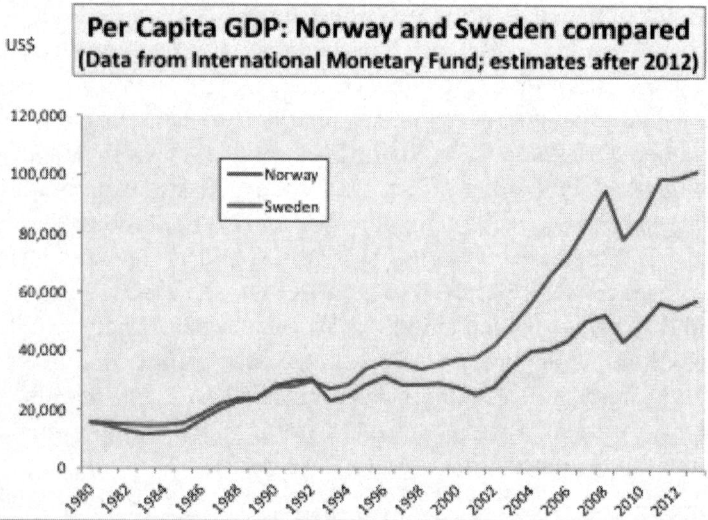

The graph compares the economies of Norway and Sweden, measuring the per capita Gross Domestic Product (GDP) – in other words, the total value of goods and services produced by a country divided by the number of inhabitants, which provides a rough guide to average income in a given year. These two countries have much in common - similar climates, low population density, high state spending on welfare and strongly export-driven economies. Norway's main export is oil, whereas Sweden's is iron ore. The per capita GDP figures were broadly similar for the period 1980-1994, but from 1995 onwards, when Sweden joined the EU, the Norwegians started to become much richer than the Swedes. Indeed, by 2008, Norway's per capita GDP, at US$ 94,815, was over 80% higher than Sweden's at US$ 52,521. It is worth pointing out Norway was already a substantial exporter of oil in 1990, several years before Sweden joined the EU, and its oil production peaked in 2001, yet the per capita GDP differential with Sweden has continued to widen. It is hard to imagine that Sweden's decision to join the EU while Norway stayed out has not been a factor. We can only wonder how much better off the UK would have been if we had followed Norway's example and retained our independence.

Chapter 6
We can make our own trading arrangements

Napoleon called us a nation of shopkeepers. Perhaps an exaggeration, but we are, and have been for many years, an outward-looking nation of businessmen and traders. One of the classic defences of free trade, *The Wealth of Nations*, was written in 1776 by a Scotsman, Adam Smith. The first General Director of the General Agreement on Tariffs and Trade (GATT), which sought to eliminate import tariffs and promote free trade across the world, was an Englishman, Sir Eric Wyndham White. In 1960, our country was one of the founder members of EFTA, the European Free Trade Association, along with Austria, Denmark, Sweden, Norway and Switzerland. In the build-up to the vote which led to the UK joining the Common Market, Edward Heath was keen to stress the benefits to British trade."British manufacturers will be selling their products in a home market five times as large as at present", claimed the 1971 Government White Paper *The United Kingdom and the European Communities*.

However, we did not move from one free trade area to another when we left EFTA to join the EEC. We joined a "Customs Union" – a group of nations which allows a certain degree of free trade among its members, while imposing common tariffs on goods imported from elsewhere. At that time it seemed a good move to reorientate our trade towards the growing economies of Western Europe. The first 25 years of GATT had not made much impact on protectionism. Most of Latin America imposed tariffs on imports from the UK. Even Commonwealth countries applied import duties on many British products. Our economy had not performed well in the previous decade and the opportunity to develop tariff-free trade links with a bloc of dynamic economies on our doorstep helped swing the vote in favour of entry.

Forty years on, the picture is very different. Thanks to the World Trade Organisation, GATT's successor, import duties worldwide are far less widespread and lower than in 1973. Furthermore, the once-dynamic economies of Western Europe are stagnating, whereas our economy has turned round considerably since the 1970s, outperforming all our European neighbours until the crisis of 2008. We would have been better off staying in EFTA, a genuine free trade area which has no parliament, no Commission and which does not require members to pay hefty contributions or surrender (or pool) of national sovereignty. It still exists, although further defections to the EU have left it with only four members – Switzerland, Norway, Iceland and Liechtenstein.

EFTA members may negotiate free trade agreements with other countries either as a bloc or as individual nations. It is left to the individual nations to decide what level of import duties (if any) they wish to apply and to what goods. This is a sharp contrast to the European Union, where free trade agreements can only be signed between the EU as a whole and another country. While it remains a member of the EU, the UK cannot, for instance, sign a free trade agreement with China or even with one of our Commonwealth friends such as New Zealand. Furthermore, if the EU decides to impose tariffs on imported foodstuffs from another country, we are obliged to apply them – and send the money to Brussels.

Should we stay locked into a declining market?

With hindsight, we backed the wrong horse 40 years ago as far as trade is concerned. The much-hyped advantages of tariff-free access to 27 European nations are starting to wane. The stagnation of their economies is already affecting our trade patterns. In May 2012, for the first time in years, more British exports were sent to countries outside the EU than to EU member states. The most recent quarterly trade statistics published at time of writing (covering the period up to March 2014) confirm this new trend, with our exports to non-EU countries exceeding those to EU member states by £0.3 billion. According to Scott Corfe and Douglas McWilliams of the Centre for Economic and Business Research, the EU is likely to become less important for UK trade in the future. They predict that in the next five years, UK exports to Asia will grow by 30%, while those to Latin America and Africa will grow by over 40% and 60% respectively. By contrast, UK exports to the EU fell from £318 billion in 2007 to £278 billion in 2012. In the final three months of 2013, a generally better year for UK business, the value of total goods exported to the EU was 6.1% lower than during the previous three months, while our exports to the rest of the world rose by 4.3% in the same period.

In reality, the amount of goods exported to the EU is less than it appears because of what is known as the Rotterdam/Antwerp distortion. A significant quantity of goods is shipped from the UK to these two large ports, one in the Netherlands and one in Belgium, some of which are in transit to another country. The country of final destination may or may not be an EU member state, but for the purposes of official statistics, they are regarded as EU exports. Ian Milne, in *A Cost Too Far* (Civitas, 2004) suggested that this results in as much as 4% of UK exports being recorded as bound for the EU which are in reality going elsewhere,

Corfe and McWilliams' study agrees with other research which suggests that the EU's trade - and not just with Britain - will continue to fall as a percentage of overall world trade. Ironically, Europe's peak, in terms of its importance to world trade, occurred in that momentous year of 1973, when it accounted for over 50% of both world imports and exports. By 2009, the EU was much larger, but it accounted for less than 42% of world trade and with the populations of Germany, Italy, Spain, Bulgaria and the Baltic States all predicted to decline in the next 50 years, the EU's share of world trade will inevitably fall further. EU regulations, in particular environmental legislation, will increasingly hamper growth. In 2000, the EU launched the "Lisbon Agenda" (not to be confused with the Lisbon

Treaty), which aimed to make the EU "the most competitive and dynamic knowledge-based economy in the world capable of sustainable economic growth with more and better jobs and greater social cohesion", by 2010. It has failed miserably, and for one basic reason: **in the EU, political considerations take priority over economics**. This is most apparent in the EU's handling of the Eurozone crisis. Departure from the Single Currency is unthinkable, even though slavish adherence to this article of faith continues to cause great financial hardship in Greece, Portugal, Spain and elsewhere.

Given all these considerations, we should therefore be most unwise to remain locked into a shrinking market for UK exports while at the same time being prevented from striking our own free trade agreements with the growing, less regulated and dynamic economies beyond Europe. Supporters of UK membership of the EU would oppose these arguments on two fronts. Firstly, they argue, the world's up-and coming economies are more interested in striking free trade deals with a large group of nations like the EU than with Britain, so it is better for us to remain within the EU. In David Cameron's words, "Of course, if Britain wanted to leave the EU we could. Then we could make trade deals with every country in the world and that is a path open to us. The argument I would make is that as part of the EU, the world's largest single market, you have the opportunity to drive some quite good deals."

Secondly, while Britain's trade with the rest of the EU may be declining, it is still too important to jeopardise. Withdrawal from the EU, we are told, would see us locked out of the EU's Single Market. Nick Clegg stated that "Investors wouldn't invest in this country because they do it because we are part of the world's largest borderless single market."

How well do the europhile arguments correspond to reality?

Firstly, looking at our trade with the rest of the world, the argument that we get better deals thanks to our EU membership is hard to substantiate. Non-EU Switzerland has been ahead of the game here compared with the EU. While negotiations are still ongoing between the EU and both Canada and Japan, Switzerland concluded free trade agreements with both countries in 2009. In May 2013, Li Keqiang, the Chinese Prime Minister, signed a free trade agreement between his country - the world's second largest economy - and the Swiss. David Cameron is keen to see an EU-China free trade agreement, but the official line from the EU is that it "is premature at the moment to discuss a free-trade agreement with China." We would therefore be better off trying to negotiate a free trade agreement as an independent country. Would the Chinese be interested? Given that the International Monetary Fund rates Switzerland as the 20th largest economy in the world, and the UK as the 6th, it is impossible to believe that they wouldn't.

Of course, David Cameron is claiming that the proposed trade agreement between the EU and the USA is the sort of "good deal" that vindicates our membership of the EU. The start of negotiations was announced on 17th June 2013 by the Prime Minister, who called it "the biggest bilateral deal in history." He claimed that the UK was likely to be the biggest beneficiary in Europe. However, starting negotiations is one thing; concluding a deal is quite another. At the June 2013 G8 summit in Northern Ireland, both Mr. Cameron and President Obama expressed the hope that the deal could be signed by the end of 2014, but there are all manner of potential obstacles, notably the French, who have insisted that TV and film industries are to be exempt from the deal. The UK's TV and film industries, which are larger than those of France, generating 6% of GDP and employing 2 million people, will therefore not reap the full benefit of any deal. The French are also likely to object to opening up their highly-protected agricultural sector to competitors. Indeed, the increase in anti-free trade MEPs in the European Parliament after May's elections, including the French *Front National*, may ultimately scupper the deal completely. Furthermore, is this likely to be a genuine free trade deal? Tory MP Douglas Carswell isn't convinced. "If this trade agreement was about letting producers on one side of the Atlantic sell goods and services to willing customers on the other, there'd not be much to negotiate", he wrote."Dig a little deeper and what is envisaged might be better described as a mercantilist arrangement, drawn up by officialdom on both sides of the Atlantic. Far from free trade with mutual standard recognition, the small print is all about common standards, which define under what conditions transatlantic trade is permitted. In order to sell something on the other side of the Atlantic, you don't just need to have a willing customer. You will need to comply with regulations drawn up by officials in both Washington and Brussels." Free trade agreements negotiated by the EU are far from ideal as they often incorporate complex trade rules devised by the United Nations. The UN wishes to enforce these onerous requirements on the whole world, including producers of goods not intended for export. Most nations wisely ignore this interference in their domestic affairs, but the EU imposes these regulations on all member states and tries to export them wherever it can. We therefore would be able to strike better, simpler and freer trade agreements, even with the USA, outside of the EU.

Trading with the Single Market

Turning now to the EU's Single Market, we must start by explaining what it actually is. It is not a free trade area, but the European Union's attempts to create an internal market where goods, capital, services and people can move between the member states without restriction - sometimes referred to as the "four freedoms." Furthermore, most EU politicians do not share the perception this side of the Channel that the Single Market is purely about trade. In 2010, Mario Monti, a former European Commissioner who later became Prime Minister of Italy, presented a paper called *A New Strategy for the Single Market*, which began with a telling quote from one of the "founding fathers" of the EU, the Belgian Paul-Henri Spaak:

"All those who, in trying to meet the economic challenges set out by the Treaty of Rome, neglected the political dimension, have failed. As long as those challenges will be addressed exclusively in an economic perspective, disregarding the political angle, we will run - I am afraid – into repeated failures."

The view of the Single Market elsewhere in the EU is that it encompasses a lot more than trade between the member states; it also includes damaging social legislation such as the Working Time Directive. The Single Market, according to our Continental friends, should be used as a vehicle for further "harmonisation" (that dreaded EU word again!), including harmonised business tax rates – a proposal which has always been opposed by the UK, as our business tax rate is lower than that of many other member states. Our support for tax competition as a means of encouraging investment and discouraging wasteful government is not shared by Brussels. In other words, as far as the rest of the EU is concerned, the Single Market does not stand for what Mrs Thatcher thought it stood for when she signed the Single European Act in 1986. It is part of the mechanism for creating a European superstate.

One often hears mention of "completing" the Single Market. This phrase also needs explanation. It means arriving at a situation where companies have unrestricted access to customers in all member states for their goods and services. The EU is a long way from reaching this point, as some member states have wished to protect parts of their service sector in particular from foreign competition. Banking, healthcare and insurance are just three of the areas subject to restrictions. The UK, which has historically been keener on free trade than some of the other member states, has been one of the strongest supporters of intra-EU trade liberalisation, but even our country imposes certain restrictions on imports from other EU member states. For example, UK citizens may not bring back unlimited quantities of alcohol from France, where alcohol duties are lower.

The Single Market, then, comes with much political baggage, and is still "incomplete" (in other words, not operating as a free trade area), particularly in the services sector, which is more important to the UK economy than to most other EU member states. So could we have our cake and eat it? In other words, could we enjoy the same degree of tariff-free trade with the EU outside the EU by striking a free trade agreement with it? In recent years, the EU has struck a number of free trade agreements with nations as diverse as Mexico,

Israel and Japan. These countries are not part of the EU, and their trade with the EU is much smaller than that between a newly-independent UK and the remaining member states would be. We therefore could do the same, gaining full access to the EU's Single Market from the outside rather than submitting to its stifling regulations There is no picking and choosing for EU member states, for the Single Market, as we have seen, is indistinguishable from the acquis communautaire – the 120,000 pages of European directives and regulations that stand as a giant monument to our politicians' folly in surrendering our right to govern ourselves. Of course, any goods we sell to the EU would still have to comply with EU standards, but this would be no different from selling goods to Japan or the USA, where the goods have to conform to Japanese or American standards respectively.

The problem with a free trade agreement with the EU is that it could take a long time to conclude. It would be much better for us when the agreements were finally signed, but the problem is how to extricate ourselves from EU membership while ensuring trade could continue without tariffs being imposed by the other 27 member states in the period immediately following independence. One possible solution is to follow the example of Norway, Iceland and Liechtenstein and remain within the European Economic Area (EEA). These countries are not in the EU and are not bound by most of its rules yet they have full free trade access to the EU. This is hardly an ideal long-term arrangement, but it might prove the least scary alterative to EU membership to put to the electorate in any referendum. It would certainly tide us over in the short term until something better could be arranged. Trade with the EU as a member of the EEA would still be subject to red tape, but considerably less red tape than if no trade agreement was in force. There would be no interruption to business and, as will be considered in more detail in the next chapter, only a minimal loss of UK jobs.

Preferential Trade with the EU can and must be preserved

We run a substantial trade deficit in goods with the EU – in other words, we buy more from them than we sell to them. The French will still wish to sell us their wine, the Germans likewise would want to preserve an important market for their cars. It is very apparent that the EU would therefore be very ill-advised to get into a trade war with a newly-independent UK as a substantial market for European exporters would be lost. This argument has been made ad nauseam by Nigel Farage and UKIP, but it is not merely wishful thinking or some mighty leap of faith with no supporting evidence. Mercedes is already expressing concern at the possibility of UK withdrawal, and David Charter, a man by no means singing from the UKIP song sheet, is sure that the company, along with others with similar concerns, will put pressure on the German government to ensure that a newly-independent UK will not be subject to the usual tariffs imposed on countries outside the EU. Ambrose Evans-Pritchard, a seasoned economic correspondent agrees, saying that, "unless the events were grotesquely mishandled.... France and Germany would bend over backwards to find a workable formula." Daniel Hannan insists that in spite of the concerns in some quarters about UK withdrawal, the EU would be happy to offer us a "privileged partnership" based on trade and not pooled sovereignty.

Adding further weight to this argument is the consideration that both the EU and the UK are both members of the World Trade Organisation, whose "overriding purpose is to help trade flow as freely as possible", according to its website, so UK withdrawal should not therefore lead to tit-for-tat trade restrictions. Also, it is stated in Article 8 of the Lisbon Treaty (to which all member states have added their signature) that,

> *1. The Union shall develop a special relationship with neighbouring countries, aiming to establish an area of prosperity and good neighbourliness, founded on the values of the Union and characterised by close and peaceful relations based on cooperation.*
>
> *2. For the purposes of paragraph 1, the Union may conclude*

specific agreements with the countries concerned. These agreements may contain reciprocal rights and obligations as well as the possibility of undertaking activities jointly.

This means that besides it being in its interests to do so, the EU would be required to seek a free trade agreement with a newly-independent UK. Article 50 of the Lisbon Treaty states that a member state wishing to leave the EU is required to give two years' notice. Whether our departure from the EU will be conducted under the auspices of Article 50 or by repealing the 1972 Accession Treaty, we will not just walk out. Some sort of notice period will be inevitable and it will not be spent just watching the clock tick away. Our trade must continue. Some trade deal must surely be one of the principal objectives for both sides during this period. Remaining in the EEA and rejoining EFTA is the simplest option and a proven formula, although some bespoke short-term transitional arrangement might be agreed instead pending a full free trade agreement. It is yet possible that some more zealous federalists may desire to give us a bloody nose when we leave, but common sense must ultimately prevail, as so many jobs on the Continent would be at stake.

Discussion about the best form of trade relationship for a newly-independent UK has thus far been largely confined to think tanks and independent analysts. With the leaders of the Labour, Conservative and Lib Dem parties all wanting us to stay in, this is hardly surprising. However, once the decision to leave has been made, the government, whether or not it actually supported independence, would have no alternative but to seek the best trading arrangement possible. Business will demand it. No one can guess at this stage which option will be chosen, but enough research has been done to prove that there are ways whereby the vital preferential access to the EU's Single Market need not be curtailed by independence. Once we have left, free from much of the damaging legislation, it is quite possible that our trade with the EU will actually improve. Swiss exports are four times higher per head of population than the UK's and Norway's are twice as high as ours which underlines the point:- you don't need to be in the EU to trade with the EU.

In summary, free of the EU, the UK will no longer have to suffer the European Commission speaking on its behalf at the World Trade Organisation, as is usually the case at the moment. Instead, we could negotiate our own free trade agreements with the rest of the world. Besides the possibility of re-joining EFTA, there is some support in the USA for our country to join the North American Free Trade Association if we became independent. In 2005, the Canadian author Brent Cameron wrote a book called *The Case for Commonwealth Free Trade*, proposing developing the Commonwealth as another free trade area. The possibilities are exciting, but we first have to leave the EU. It is absurd for supporters of EU membership to say withdrawal would make us more inward-looking. The truth is that, once we are out, it would become far easier for us to reorientate our trade towards the growing economies of the world.

Chapter 7
Leaving the EU would boost employment for UK-born workers

In Chapter 4, we considered the origins of the so-called "three million jobs" myth. If only the many politicians who have parroted this nonsense ad nauseam had checked the data from the Government's own Office for National Statistics, they would soon have discovered their error. Fortunately, Professor Tim Congdon, the former Chairman of The Freedom Association has done their homework for them, showing in his 2013 booklet *Europe Doesn't Work* that the EU has actually *destroyed* British jobs. Most of the statistics in the next few paragraphs are taken from this source.

This chapter considers two issues. Firstly, the hard facts proving that EU membership has destroyed, rather than created, jobs for UK-born workers and secondly, a repudiation of the scaremongering about widespread job losses were Britain to regain its independence.

UK employment since 1973 – what the statistics really say

At the start of 1973, when the UK joined the EEC, there were 24.9 million people in employment. By the first quarter of 1983, the figure had fallen below 23.7 million - a drop of 1.2 million, or nearly 5%. This hardly suggests that our membership of the Common Market was beneficial for employment. The statistics for UK-born men in employment are even more interesting. In 1973, there were 15.6 million men at work, 14 million in 1983 and 13.8 million in 1993, the year that the EEC became the European Union.

In 1993, the UK was beginning its recovery from the recession of 1990-91 and was to enjoy almost a decade and a half of growth before the downturn known as the Great Recession, which began in 2007. However, by 2007, a significant change had taken place in the UK labour marker. Three years earlier, the EU had enlarged eastwards to take in eight countries which had been under Marxist rule since the end of the Second World War:- Poland, Hungary, the Czech Republic, Slovenia, Slovakia, Estonia, Latvia and Lithuania (often referred to as "EU8"). These countries were much poorer than the nations of the West and, unsurprisingly, many of their workers were keen to take advantage of one of the four freedoms of the EU's Single Market – free movement of people – to take a job in a Western European country where wages were higher than in their native countries. Fearing a disruption of their workforce by a sudden influx of cheap labour, France, Germany and Austria, among others, applied the permitted short-term restrictions on free movement. The UK did not. Tony Blair, Prime Minister at the time, latched on to a report by a German think tank which calculated that a mere 15,000 Eastern European workers would travel to the UK. This estimate proved to be spectacularly wrong, with 653,000 immigrants arriving from these countries between 2004 and 2011.

This mass movement of people has had a significant effect on the UK labour market, which has been particularly noticeable since the start of the Great Recession. In the 12 months to mid-2009, some 800,000 jobs were lost. Two years later, there were still 800,000 fewer UK-born people in employment than at the end of 2007, but the number of people in employment from the EU8 countries actually rose by 200,000. This suggests that **allowing free movement from these countries has actually resulted in a loss of jobs for UK-born workers.** It is not as if most of the arrivals from the EU8 countries were highly-skilled individuals such as surgeons or financiers. According to a report for the Office of National Statistics covering the period 2007-09, 37.5% of EU8-born workers are employed in "elementary occupations". 25.4% work in manufacturing and 29.2% in distribution, hotels and restaurants. In other words, workers from these countries are taking unskilled jobs which any UK born person could do. Tim Congdon quotes a report by Professor David Metcalf of the Migration Advisory Committee which calculated that 160,000 more UK-born people would have been in work if there had been no migration from outside the EU between 2005 and 2010 instead of the 700,000 who did arrive. When asked directly to confirm this, he replied, "Yes, that would be a reasonable way of putting it." It is therefore not unreasonable, argues Tim Congdon, to apply a similar formula to the 588,000 migrants from the EU (not just EU8 countries) who arrived in the same period. This would result in their arrival causing a net loss of 135,000 jobs for UK residents.

Even allowing for the willingness of workers from the EU8 countries to work unsociable hours, the shortages of suitable UK-born staff in fields such as nursing and the extra business generated by some of these people which has not resulted in any loss of employment for UK nationals, (such as the many specialist Polish food shops which would not exist without the large Polish diaspora), the bottom line is that the Government's own statistics prove that 40 years of membership of the EU has actually **destroyed** jobs for the UK resident population. Indeed, British jobs were being lost before the arrival of the workers from the EU8 countries. Our fishing industry was decimated by the Common Fisheries Policy, which forced us to open up our rich waters to fishing vessels from other EU member states. In the decade between 1995 and 2005, over 6,000 fishing jobs were lost – nearly one third of all UK fishermen. EU regulation has hit small businesses especially hard. Danny Winter, who lives in Gloucestershire, ran a company whose main business was nail polish filling. The EU's Cosmetic Labelling Directive, which required him to obtain a "doctor's certificate" for each product, costing £160, forced him to close it. "This was OK for the larger firms, who do massive runs, but for small firms it was unviable", said Danny. "For nail polishes that had been around for 100 years, it was totally unnecessary, but Trading Standards were zealous in their work, and took everything literally." Danny's story is typical of businessmen up and down the country.

Not all UK industry supports EU membership

Going back to the "three million jobs" myth, a rough calculation suggests that the figure is actually too low. More than four million jobs are tied up in trade with the European Union. The overall UK workforce was very slightly under 30 million in November 2013, and over 32% of UK GDP – in other words, the total value of goods and services produced by a country – was exported. As was noted in the previous chapter, the percentage of UK exports bound for the EU fell below 50% in 2012 and looks like it will continue to fall, but if we say that 15% of UK GDP is tied up with exporting to the EU and therefore 15% of the workforce, this works out at roughly 4.5 million.

This means that the majority of the workforce would not suffer in the slightest if we left. Free from the EU, we would still need to have some business regulation, but it need not (and almost certainly will not) be as onerous as at present. There would be no political motive to "harmonise" everything, so UK manufacturers would not have to put the dreaded CE mark on goods for domestic use. With less regulation, businesses could expand and thus take on more workers, while an independent UK, free to strike its own free trade deals with the rest of the world (or as part of EFTA), would be able to increase its exports to the growing economies of the world.

Given that only 15% of UK jobs are tied up with exporting to the EU, it is not logical for nearly 40% of firms surveyed in a recent opinion poll to suggest that withdrawal followed by a trade agreement would have a negative impact. In reality, the business community is sharply divided. An opinion poll in December 2013 saw a fairly even split on whether to vote in or out in any referendum, with 38% of businessmen believing the UK economy would be better off if Britain left the EU versus 31% who said the economy would suffer. Small businesses are, as a rule, the most enthusiastic about withdrawal from the EU – support was as high as 67% in a poll of taken in 2011. One of the many businessmen supporting withdrawal for economic rather than political reasons is Rollo Reid, who runs Reidsteel, a company based in Christchurch, Dorset which exports steel across the world. "The cancer of EU regulations", he says, is "killing off our economy.

We are told we have to belong to a big club to work in the BRICs (i.e., Brazil, Russia, India and China) and elsewhere. Nonsense; the last thing we need to compete in the real world is crushingly expensive EU regulation. We are told these regulations are needed to access the much vaunted 'Single Market'. There is no Single Market in Europe; even when we get an order from Europe, protectionism stops us from working." For employees in companies like Reidsteel, leaving the EU would certainly not result in redundancies, nor for those working in a hardware store in a small town in Herefordshire or for a nurseryman in Gloucestershire, both of whom spontaneously expressed their frustration at the burden of EU legislation to your author during the past year, without knowing his views in the subject beforehand!

Small firms inevitably suffer more from EU regulation. Suppose two competing companies are affected by the same piece of legislation. It may require them both to devote 20 man days to studying the legislation, producing an impact assessment and devising an implementation strategy. This will obviously be much less disruptive for a company with 200 employees than for one with only 10 employees. It therefore is hardly surprising that big business tends to be supportive of EU membership. A company which is large enough to devote only a small percentage of its overall manpower to compliance issues can use EU regulation as a means of preserving its share of the market against a small company without the same resources. And as long as we remain in the EU, the flood of legislation will continue. A recent regulation, EU No. 305/2011, which came into force in 2013, insists that every item used in construction has to display a CE mark. One small fabricator in the UK which employs 20 people is considering shutting the business down because of the implementation costs. It is probably not the only company in this position. Essentially, the burden of legislation acts as a deterrent to competition, which is ultimately bad for jobs, as competition is a spur to innovation and growth.

Would the big firms really pull out?

Business support for our EU membership is not confined to firms big enough to influence EU legislation to their benefit and thus disadvantage their competitors. Unsurprisingly, companies who have taken advantage of cheap Eastern European labour are unenthusiastic about UK withdrawal. In August 2013, both Next and Tesco were accused by Labour's Chris Bryant of favouring Polish employees over UK-born staff. Both companies denied the charges and a spokesman from Next claimed that Polish workers were taken on because insufficient UK-born staff could be found.

The other issue which concerns senior management in large companies is whether withdrawal would disadvantage existing business in Europe if access to the Single Market were lost. Given that the EU has not so far included services in its free trade deals, anxiety in the City of London appears understandable. Unlike much of the UK economy, the City runs a trade surplus with the EU, so the argument that withdrawal would hurt the EU more than the UK does not apply here. However, a survey of business in the City, undertaken by TheCity UK in 2008-9 concluded that by far the largest category of businesses in the City came into what it called the "hard to impossible to leave" category, so in spite of much huffing and puffing, they would stay regardless. In the main, European banks with a substantial presence in London are the keenest on EU membership. This is understandable, but for most financiers, withdrawal ought to be beneficial, as it is all too apparent that there is little love for the Square Mile in Brussels, as we saw in Chapter 5. Changes to European voting rules in November could mean the City facing a coalition with a built-in majority hostile to its interests. David Cameron has already had to push very hard to tone down EU financial legislation which would adversely affect the City more than any other part of the EU. He has not always been successful. The removal of any exemption for the City from the damaging Financial Transaction Tax, following a ruling by judges at the European Court of Justice, is a flavour of what is to come if we remain within the EU. There is no doubt that the City would survive and flourish following withdrawal, especially as regulation could be repatriated. Gerard Lyons, the chief economic advisor to London's mayor Boris Johnson and former chief economist of Standard Chartered Bank, said the City of London's success was "not dependent" upon the UK remaining part of the EU, while Sir Nigel Wicks, the chairman of the British Bankers Association, added, "If the City did not exist...where else in Europe would it be? Now, I have respect for Paris, I have respect for Frankfurt, but I do not for one moment see them being able to replicate what we have in London," Some key City figures are among a significant number of influential figures in the business world who support outright withdrawal. These include Howard Shore of Shore Capital and Helena Morrisey, chief Executive of Newton Investment Management, one of the top women in the City.

It is also unlikely that big manufacturing companies would pull out. Carlos Ghosn, Chief Executive of Nissan, hit the headlines in November 2013, stating that his company was prepared to reconsider its future plans and investment in the UK if we voted to leave, Lord Stoddart of Swindon recalls similar scare stories nearly 40 years ago. "As the then MP for Swindon," he said, "I can well remember the Chief Executive of British Leyland, Sir Donald Stokes, writing to all his employees in my constituency telling them that they could lose their jobs if they did not vote to stay in the EEC in the 1975 referendum. He said the British car industry would be lost if we left. The British people did vote to stay in and what happened? We lost the British car industry anyway. Sir Donald later recanted his statement, admitting that he had been wrong. The lesson from this is that bully boys should always be resisted." Lord Stoddart also pointed out that Nissan was a strong advocate of Britain's membership of the Eurozone in the late 1990s. Nissan's Sunderland plant is therefore likely to survive our independence.

Renegotiation from within is unrealistic

Top management of large multinationals are not the sort of people with the time or the inclination to study the detailed research showing that it is possible – indeed very likely – that access to the Single

Market would be unaffected by withdrawal. They just want to ensure that their businesses are run profitably and are concerned about the uncertainties created by the withdrawal debate, even though many of them are equally concerned about the damaging effects of EU legislation. 70% of finance managers, for instance, want the UK government to renegotiate the EU treaties to safeguard the City of London, and 68% support the repatriation of some powers of financial regulation from Brussels. There is an obvious attraction for such men in securing a deal which returned powers to the UK and reduced red tape rather than outright withdrawal, as this would be less disruptive or unpredictable.

However, the items in any shopping list given by, for example, the Business for Britain campaign to David Cameron when he attempts either to return powers to the UK or to lead a campaign for a change of direction for the EU as a whole are likely to be rejected by other member states and the European Commission, Ironically, the success of eurosceptic parties in the May 2014 European Parliamentary elections has made Cameron's job harder as supporters of the EU project have closed ranks. His opposition to the arch-federalist Jean-Claude Juncker's becoming President of the European Commission has only further isolated him and inflamed anti-British feeling. Cameron was right when he said that the Commission "is so obsessed with red tape that it believes that removing regulations which damage businesses is an act of self-harm," but to many in the Commission removing regulations, let alone repatriating powers to the member states, is tantamount to undoing the whole EU project. The desire to create a federal superstate has not been buried by May's elections. David Cameron criticised his opponents within the Conservative Party for "throwing in the towel" - in other words, viewing renegotiation as a pointless exercise, but their cynicism has been vindicated by the Juncker saga.

To reiterate a point, no advocates of reforming the EU are proposing strangling the source of this legislation which UK businesses find so damaging – in other words, abolishing the Commission. It will continue churning out regulations in its top-heavy manner which is so much at odds with our approach to trade and business.

We therefore have to put up with it or leave. Let's leave, especially given there are further reasons why withdrawal need not be feared as far as the UK job market is concerned. As we saw in the previous chapter, one of the main tasks during the inevitable transition period before independence would be to ensure that trade continues. If no better alternative can be devised, continued EEA membership at least would preserve our access to the single market and thus any jobs dependent on exports to the EU.

Furthermore, the factors that have attracted foreign investors will not be affected. Big companies are not drawn to the UK primarily because of our membership of the EU. A survey by the Financial Times in 2012 found that, whereas some 50% of foreign investors chose the UK because it was an English-speaking country with access to the EU, 90% said that their top reason for choosing the UK was to service the UK market. The UK will continue to be a business-friendly country. In 2012 we ranked No. 7 in the World Bank's "Ease of Doing Business" table of 183 nations, higher than any other EU member state except Denmark. We have a less regulated labour market and, in spite of the EU's legislative burden, we still place less red tape in the way of new businesses than other member states. Furthermore, English is the language of world trade. We would retain these benefits on independence – indeed, we can lighten the regulatory burden and increase workforce flexibility still further once we are in the position to repeal EU legislation such as the Working Time Directive or the Agency Workers' Directive (which makes the employment of casual staff less viable). Furthermore, we would still be well-placed geographically. Being midway between US and Asian time zones is a great benefit to City financiers. This would not change on independence. It is most unfortunate that every time Nick Clegg opens his mouth, some fool speaks. His remark that there is "nothing bulldog about Britain hovering somewhere in the Mid-Atlantic" is pretty sad, even by his standards. Someone need to tell him gently that no one advocating withdrawal from the EU is seriously considering a physical relocation of our country. Calais will still be only 21 miles from Dover when we regain our independence! We should therefore continue to enjoy easy access to the EU for our goods via the traditional ferry ports, the new London Gateway port and the Channel Tunnel.

Where some jobs may be lost

This positive assessment of employment prospects in the UK outside of the EU does not rule out the possibility of some job losses. Political pressure may result in some European banks scaling down their operations in the City of London and other investment banks relocating their European business to within the Eurozone. Goldman Sachs warned in December 2013 that it may do just that. Given the mobility of the financial sector, this should not be a cause for concern on the jobs front. It is hard to imagine former employees of the company popularly known as "Golden Sacks" because of the size of their staff bonuses sitting outside supermarkets selling copies of the *Big Issue!* UK companies might find themselves outside the EU-wide tendering process for European government contracts and thus be forced to shed jobs, but conversely, the UK government would then need no longer be required to obey EU rules on tendering. Some companies may indeed up sticks and relocate to an EU member state, but probably very few.

In summary, at this stage we cannot be absolutely certain that no job will be lost on withdrawal, but there should not be many if negotiations are handled well. Even the most pessimistic serious estimate, written over a decade ago and thus before the implementation of much of the most damaging legislation, came up with a figure far below the job losses in the 2008-9 downturn and an independent UK government would have far more tools at its disposal to counter any economic downturn – the money saved from the UK's direct contribution, the ability to repeal regulations damaging to British industry and the possibility of implementing a real "British jobs for British workers" policy in certain sectors of the economy if needed. The claim by the pro-EU British Influence group that over

1½ million jobs would be lost is not supported by any detailed study. Some jobs **may** be lost, but it would only be a short-term blip, and others **will** be created. It is likely that with small businesses being the main beneficiaries of exit the balance of employment may shift in the short term from larger to smaller companies. For instance, free from the Common Fisheries Policy, our fishing industry would certainly revive, creating thousands of new jobs. By contrast, at this stage, the only certain job losses are fairly small in number. UK citizens employed at the EU institutions based in Britain – the European Banking Agency, the European Medicines Agency and the European Police College – would lose their jobs; the UK Commissioner, whoever it might be when we leave, will have to learn to adjust to life without a six-figure salary. Likewise our 73 MEPs, currently earning €84,000 per year plus generous expenses, will find themselves redundant, as will, among others, over 1,000 staff who work for the European Commission, 150 who work for the European External Action Service and almost 400 who work in the European Parliament while the UK's civil service can be cut back as, even if we stayed in the EEA and thus had to implement a limited number of EU laws, there would still be far fewer of them to transpose onto our nation's statute book. How tragic!

Chapter 8
We could keep the lights on

Anyone listening to any Radio 4 BBC news bulletin on 19th February 2013 would have heard experts from the energy watchdog OFGEM expressing their concern about our energy supply. Their worries revolved around the closure of a number of coal-fired power stations by the end of 2015 without sufficient alternative energy sources being available to replace them. Energy prices were likely to rise further and even this might not save us from power shortages.

To any listener, there would have been an obvious solution to the problem – postpone the closure of these power stations until the energy shortfall can be made up. Typically, however, the BBC's reporting did not mention the reason for the closure of our coal-fired stations - the EU's Large Combustible Plant Directive (2001/80/EC). This piece of legislation gave an ultimatum to any power station licensed before July 1987. Either it must be adapted to comply with EU emissions targets for sulphur dioxide, the nitrogen oxides and dust or else it could only be operated for a further 20,000 hours and must close completely by the end of 2015. So far, six of the nine power stations which do not meet these requirements have already been closed. It is hardly surprising that a report written for National Grid as far back as 2007 stated that this Directive presented "a number of challenges to generators and National Grid." Six years later, National Grid was using stronger language, warning of possible blackouts in the event of a cold snap, as 95% of the available generating capacity would be required to meet demand.

The knights in shining green armour

If the BBC tries to avoid playing down the European Union's role in our energy supply problems, the EU itself is less reticent, loudly trumpeting its claim to be in the forefront of the "green" agenda. As David Charter puts it, the EU rediscovered "its purpose in a new century to lead the world out of carbon darkness into the renewable light." However, given the dog's dinner the EU has made of dealing with the Eurozone crisis, it is quite laughable to imagine that its bureaucrats, like a group of knights in shining green armour, are somehow capable saving the planet! Take, for instance, the emissions trading scheme. This set up a system of permits to emit Carbon Dioxide (CO_2) which energy-using companies could buy and sell. This flagship policy has proved a failure, as an over-allocation of permits in the period immediately before the Great Recession caused their price to plummet to the point where the whole scheme became worthless.

The EU has also caused much hardship because of its enthusiasm for biofuels, decreeing that 5.75% of the fuel used in the transport sector should come from renewable sources by 2010. Many farmers, particularly in the developing world, promptly switched from growing food to growing fuel. Unfortunately, this has led to food shortages. As the poverty action group Action Aid International pointed out, "When staple food crops are diverted to produce fuel, prices rise. These rising prices have in turn hit import-dependent developing countries hard." Oxfam has come out against setting biofuel targets beyond 2020, claiming it has resulted not just in rising food prices but also in land grabs and evictions.

However, the EU continues to go its own sweet way, pressing ahead with plans to introduce its "E10" petrol, so named because it will contain 10% bio-ethanol. Motoring experts reckon that this less efficient fuel will result in motorists having to pay £200 extra per year on petrol costs, with small economical cars suffering the biggest loss of efficiency.

Yet another example of the EU backing the wrong horse has been its enthusiasm for wind power. Of all the forms of renewable energy, wind power is one of the most unreliable and consequently the most expensive. As Roger Helmer, UKIP's energy spokesman explains:-

"It's increasingly clear that intermittent renewables don't deliver. The power generated and the emissions savings, are largely offset by the inefficiencies inherent in running fossil fuel generation intermittently as back-up to complement wind. Wind power is not only desecrating our countryside – it's also failing to deliver, even in its own terms. This was brought home to me in the Brussels parliament on Feb. 20th, when I heard a presentation on "Capacity Payments". These are, quite simply, massive payments – billions of Euros – which will be made to gas-fired operators just to keep their capacity "available" – and largely idle, on spinning reserve – waiting until the wind drops and their output is needed. We knew that wind farm operators were paid for doing nothing when the wind was too strong, or when their capacity was not needed. Now we'll also be paying for the wasteful operation of fossil fuel backup."

But the EU presses on regardless. The so-called 20-20-20 targets aim for 20% of energy to come from renewable sources by 2020, with CO_2 emissions reduced by 20% of the 1990 level. The Department of Business has estimated that it will cost the UK £22 billion to meet these targets. Looking further ahead, the EU was aiming to cut CO_2 emissions in member states by between 80% and 95% of their 1990 levels by 2050, even though its favourite form of renewable energy is doing little to reduce CO_2 emissions, because of the need for a backup. This target seems very unrealistic and a recent European Commission document, the "Climate and energy framework to 2030", appears finally to have recognised that high energy costs across the EU are making businesses uncompetitive. There were no renewables targets set for individual member states, even though there will be an overall EU-wide binding renewable energy target of 27%. Regrettably, the 2020 targets remain unchanged.

Environmental legislation is damaging industry......

Roger has also provided the explanation for some recent events which also, at first glance, seem very strange. Given the handsome profits made by the oil industry worldwide, why did the oil refinery at Coryton, Essex close down recently, while Grangemouth in Scotland only narrowly escaped a similar fate? The answer lies once again with proposed EU legislation – in particular, the Emissions Trading Scheme Phase III, the Industrial Emissions Directive, and the Fuel Quality Directive. Refineries in the UK work on a margin of around 1.65p per litre. Once operating costs, energy and salaries are deducted, that comes down to a net figure of 0.6p per litre. The Fuel Quality Directive alone will cost 1p per litre. All these regulatory costs, when added together, will erode the tiny profit margin for oil refiners and instead see the industry making a loss of around 0.75p per litre. Consequently, it is becoming cheaper to import refined oil products from other countries than to refine under EU rules in this country. No one looking to invest in refining capacity will choose a location in the EU because of the with massive and growing regulatory costs.

Meanwhile, the high energy costs of EU environmental legislation have closed down the UK's aluminium smelters and threaten other intensive energy users, such as our cement and chemical industries, which face being rendered uncompetitive. A news story in the Sunday Times on 6th February 2011 remarked that "Leading chemical companies have warned the government that its energy policies will render them uncompetitive, leaving plants to 'die on the vine', to quit Britain for lower-cost countries." The three most recent energy secretaries have all been guilty of spectacular misjudgements which made the problem particularly acute for the UK. Ed Miliband, Chris Huhne and Ed Davey all assumed that oil and gas prices were going to continue to rise, making renewables, especially wind power, an economically viable option. Thanks to the fracking revolution in the USA and the recent rehabilitation of oil-producing Iran on the world stage, the opposite has happened, leaving our country locked into commitments to expensive and inefficient sources of renewable energy in order to meet the 20-20-20 target.

The degree to which industry (and consumers) right across the EU are suffering from the legacy of these madcap policies is remarkable. Electricity prices for the EU's industrial consumers are currently more than double those in the US and Russia, and 20% higher than in China. The situation with gas prices is worse; they are four times higher than comparable US, Canadian, Indian or Russian tariffs and 12% higher than in China. No wonder the recovery from the recent recession has been so lacklustre in most of the EU.

....and all in the name of dubious science....

For all the EU's failures with its renewable energy policy, its idealism has been defended on the grounds that man-made global warming threatens the planet. However, is this true? Confidence in both the impartiality of scientific research on this subject and its accuracy has been declining, especially since the so-called "Climategate" scandal of 2009, when a hacker leaked a series of e-mails from scientists in the Climate Research Unit of the University of East Anglia, including a long discussion of how to marginalise those dissenters who did not agree with the so-called "consensus" on global warming. The contents of some of the leaked e-mails are quite astonishing. They included an alleged note from Professor Phil Jones, the director of the university's Climatic Research Unit to an American colleague describing the death of a sceptic as "cheering news"; along with a suggestion that a "trick" is to be used to "hide the decline" in temperature. Another e-mail from an American academic to Professor Jones said: "Next time I see Pat Michaels (a climate change sceptic) at a scientific meeting, I'll be tempted to beat the xxxx out of him. Very tempted."

It is remarkable that the fallout from these revelations has not been greater, but scepticism is definitely on the rise and not just because of the deplorable behaviour of some climate scientists. For example, if it is beyond doubt that the world is going to get warmer, why have climate scientists come up with so many conflicting predictions as to how much warmer? As Jamie Whyte points out, "If known physical laws entailed climate models, there would be only one climate model, not dozens." Furthermore, as many of these models have proved unreliable in making short term predictions, how can they be trusted to predict the long-term future ? More than a decade after apocalyptic tales of looming global catastrophe first emerged, figures from the

Met Office have actually shown that there has been no statistically significant increase in the world's temperature since 1997.

....and even more dubious politics

One thing is very clear. Whether or not the world really is facing environmental problems in the future, the EU's actions are not going to make any difference. A year ago, it was reported that China and India between them were building over 800 coal-fired power stations. EU demands for the UK to phase out our nine power stations that failed to meet emissions targets are a drop in the ocean by comparison. It is utterly pointless for the EU to pat itself on the back for being so virtuous while businesses are suffering and pensioners are shivering – and all for no tangible benefit. It is hard to know whether most EU politicians really believe in global warming or whether they support green legislation because of the opportunities it provides to increase both the power of the EU and their countries' tax revenue. As far back as November 20th 2000, Jacques Chirac, the then French President, claimed during a speech at The Hague that the United Nations' Kyoto Protocol, which commits all those countries who ratified it to internationally binding emission reduction targets, represented "the first component of an authentic global governance." One further reason why we must be sceptical of the motives of EU politicians is their behaviour in attempting to impose heavy tariffs on solar panels imported from China in 2013. Why restrict sales of a form of renewable energy which could indeed cut carbon emissions? The answer is that the cheapness of Chinese solar panels was threatening European manufacturers - in other words, protectionist forces were allowed to triumph over the EU's apparent commitment to greening the environment.

The prospects for an independent UK

For all the cynicism we may feel about the motives of politicians or the impartiality of scientists whose livelihoods in many cases are dependent on funding by governments ideologically committed to reducing CO_2 emissions, there is no doubt that the development of renewable energy sources will be essential at some time in the future. Supplies of coal and oil are finite and will run out one day, even though "fracking" has made available considerably larger quantities of the latter than was believed possible 20 years ago. Unfortunately, as a member of the EU, the UK finds itself locked into an ideologically- and politically-driven energy agenda which does not operate in the best interest of either its citizens or its industries.

Our politicians, it has to be admitted to their shame, have been as keen as any in Europe to jump on the "green" bandwagon, offering a generous subsidy to landowners to erect wind farms. Given that one of the beneficiaries has been the Prime Minister's father-in-law, it is hard not to be sceptical about their motives. What is especially unfair is that the "generous subsidy" is an extra tax paid by all of us, whether rich and poor, on top of our already astronomical fuel bills, to benefit people who are often pretty wealthy anyway.

Alongside the "Climategate" scandal, the bitterly cold winter of 2010 and the coldest spring for 50 years in 2013 have further changed public attitudes in the UK. Green taxes are losing popular support in the face of possible blackouts and increasing energy costs which are already well above international prices. There can be no change in direction as long as the Liberal Democrats play a part in the government, as they are keen supporters of green taxes and therefore of higher energy bills, but the suffering public have had enough.

Unfortunately, even in a future Lib Dem-free government, there can also be no radical change of policy unless we leave the EU. Even such freedom as the Government thought it enjoyed to subsidise the back-up gas-fired power stations which are needed when the windmills won't turn looks likely to fall foul of the European Commission. This is another case of EU politics triumphing over common sense, as the Commission claims that this subsidy would damage its desire to create a single EU market in energy. Why bother? Its alternative suggestion was that the UK should import excess energy supply from the continent. The Commission is also threatening to interfere with the UK government's plan to build a new nuclear reactor at Hinkley Point in Somerset on the grounds that the deal may breach EU state aid rules.

Of course, the degree to which an independent UK will escape the straitjacket of damaging green legislation depends on the calibre of the politicians elected after withdrawal. It is hard to imagine, however, even in a worst case scenario that the energy problems affecting the UK would be so critical, for the opportunities outside the EU to address these issues are considerable. We can end the dithering which is pushing our current generating capacity to its limit. Even the pro-EU Open Europe think tank has admitted that the underinvestment in energy generation capacity in the UK, which could result in blackouts, has been "caused by a changing regulatory environment led by unrealistic and contradictory EU climate policies." In an independent UK these uncertainties would disappear. We could pursue clean coal technology or "fracking," which would cut energy costs, but are not favoured in Brussels. We could also withdraw from the Kyoto Protocol, just as the Canadians did in 2011, an affirmation of the ancient principle that no government can bind its successor. This would enable us to abandon the dash for wind and focus our attention on other forms of renewable energy which are more effective and less unsightly, such as geothermal energy or tidal power. We could then also scrap gimmicky and unrealistic targets for renewable energy such as 20-20-20, instead allowing time for any form of renewable energy to be sufficiently developed to the point where it becomes cost-effective, rather than having to rely on subsidies such as "green levies".

One thing is clear – freedom to determine our own energy policy would not only boost the UK economy by between 1¾% and 2½% of GDP, but would actually save lives. The rise in fuel prices has forced many people, including the most vulnerable, to cut back on heating their homes in the winter, resulting in confirmed hypothermia deaths in the UK almost doubling from 135 in 2006/7 to 260 in 2010/11, with 1,876 in total requiring hospital treatment. Most of these victims were pensioners, some of whom would have fought to preserve our country's independence in the Second World War. How tragic that, having survived the conflict with Adolf Hitler, they have been killed off by our own government's craven subservience to the unrealistic ideology of a foreign power.

Chapter 9
We could control our borders

On 20th April 1968, the Conservative Shadow Secretary of State for Defence delivered a speech in Birmingham on the subject of immigration. As Enoch Powell had obtained a first class honours degree in classics at Cambridge University, an allusion to the Roman poet Virgil in his speech should not have attracted much attention. Unfortunately, the phrase he used, "Like the Roman, I seem to see 'the River Tiber foaming with much blood'", was manipulated by the press, who subsequently referred to the speech as the "Rivers of Blood" speech. It caused such a furore that Powell was dismissed from the Shadow Cabinet, in spite of the overwhelming support he received from the general public. Only 800 out of 100,000 letters he received disagreed with him and 300 of 412 Conservative Party constituency associations supported him.

The enduring legacy of Powell's speech has been a taboo about questioning the benefit of immigration, which only now is slowly being broken. Meanwhile, in the intervening years, immigration into the UK has accelerated and the more immigrants have arrived, the more uneasy the native UK population has become. A hardening of attitude was particularly noticeable during the New Labour years (1997-2010), when the number of people who considered that "immigration and race relations" was the most important issue facing the UK rose from 5% to 40%. Although Victoria Ayling, a UKIP councillor, insisted in December 2013 that she was only referring to illegal immigrants when she talked about "sending the lot back" in a video, an Ipsos Mori poll commissioned while Labour was in power found that 49% of people felt that immigrants – and not just illegal immigrants - should be encouraged to return to their country of origin.

A poll for Sky News in October 2013 suggests opinions have hardened further. It found more than two thirds of the British public believe the UK population is too large, while the same percentage (67%) of those questioned said the coalition's attempt to reduce net migration to 100,000 a year was not sufficient and that more should be done. More than a quarter of those polled (27%) believe the wave of immigration Britain has experienced in the last decade has brought no positive benefit to the nation, and more than half (52%) say they would be more likely to vote for a party that promises "significantly" to reduce the level of migration. The most recent migration statistics, published in February 2014, will only add to these concerns. No fewer than 532,000 migrants arrived in the year to September 2013, an increase of 35,000 on the previous 12 months. Migration from the EU rose from 149,000 to 209,000.

In spite of all-too-frequent calls to "embrace diversity" from politicians, particularly Labour MPs, the government's own statistics explain why many of us feel so concerned. At the time of the 2001 census, the UK's population stood at just over 59 million. By the time of the next census 10 years later, our crowded little island contained 63 million people, and the population is projected to reach over 70 million by 2030. Longer term projections are even more frightening. The Office of National Statistics has warned that if immigration continues at recent levels, the population of UK could well rise above 100 million in 100 years' time. In the year between mid-2011 and mid-2012 alone, the population of the UK grew by 0.7%. Much of this growth was fuelled either by immigration or foreign-born mothers having children. Without the immigration of recent years, the UK population would be more or less static and there would be far less pressure on our countryside, housing, schools and healthcare – issues of increasing concern to many, who feel not just that our traditional hospitality is being abused, but that, to quote Margaret Thatcher, we are being "swamped."

Of course, immigration occurs from many countries and is not solely a European Union issue. Indeed, the immigrant group which attracts the most hostility – the Muslim community – consists largely of people born outside the EU, with 69% originating from the Indian sub-continent. However, two points need to be made. Firstly, the Muslim community may be the largest and often the most visible immigrant group in large and medium-sized towns and cities, but the largest and most audible immigrant group in smaller towns comes from an EU member state – namely Poland. Secondly and most importantly, while EU member states retain the power to restrict immigration from outside the EU (even though many people feel our government is not doing enough), free movement of people within the member states is one of the four "freedoms" of the EU's Single Market. In other words, as long as we remain within the EU, we cannot exercise total control of our borders. David Cameron's pledge to reduce total net immigration (the number of people coming to the UK minus the number of people leaving) to less than 100,000 by 2015 is proving unachievable because of our membership of the EU. The Free Movement Directive 2004/38/EC sets the rules. It does not allow unconditional free movement. A national of an EU member state must reside for a continuous period of five years to gain the right of "permanent residence" in that member state. Until then, a national of an EU member state and his/her family can reside for up to three months in another member state provided that they do not become an "unreasonable burden" on the social assistance system of the country they move to. After three months, the person will have to prove that he/she has a job in that country, is a student or has "sufficient resources" to keep living there without becoming a burden.

However, the Directive provides for a series of exceptions restricting national governments' ability to expel people who do not meet these requirements. For example, a national of an EU member state who moves to the UK to find a job can remain in the UK for more than three months if this person can prove that he/she is continuing to seek employment and has "a genuine chance" of finding work. Family members of EU citizens - regardless of whether they are EU citizens or not - are also granted certain rights, including access to social assistance. This has caused particular resentment in the UK, as our welfare state includes many non-contributory, means-tested benefits, making it more generous than that of some other EU member states which are more contribution-based. Some access is restricted by a "right to reside" test, but this restriction has been challenged by the European Commission, which regarded it as discriminatory.

Theresa May, the Home Secretary, recently attempted to persuade the EU to place limits on this particular single market "freedom" but was told in no uncertain terms by Viviane Reding, the EU Justice Commissioner, that "our EU rules are good and they are here to stay." William Hague, the fromer Foreign Secretary, said earlier this year that any pledge to impose restrictions would be "undeliverable." Mrs May's action smacks more of desperation in the face of public resentment than any principled change of heart. David Cameron is not facing any pressure from businesses to end the principle of free movement of people, even those seeking reform in other areas. Lord Wolfson, the CEO of Next and one of the first 400 registered supporters of the Business for Britain campaign, which seeks a relationship within the EU "based on trade, not politics," said in November 2013 that, "in place of the deeply-undesirable goal of ever-increasing political union, the EU must have a new simple clear objective – Free trade; the unimpeded movement of goods, services, capital **and people**." (Author's emphasis)

Why Romania and Bulgaria may mark the tipping point

The influx of immigrants from the Central and Eastern European countries which joined the EU in 2004 was far greater than official government estimates at the time. It still causes resentment. "The feel of the town has changed", said a lady ringing in to Radio 4's *Any Answers* from a rural area of East Anglia in November 2013. Another caller expressed concern about English-speakers being in a minority in a class at her village primary school because of the large number of Polish families in the area. A few minutes later, another caller rang in to support the Poles. An older man, he recalled the bravery of Polish pilots in the Second World War, who were particularly skilled at deflecting the German V2 "doodlebug" rockets with the wings of their planes, ensuring that far fewer of them landed in residential areas. However, he was missing the point. Thanks to the number of Poles now living in the UK, the positive image of brave Polish airmen in the war or the courageous Lech Walesa and his Solidarity trade union standing up to the totalitarian Soviet-backed régime in 1981 is being superseded by a more negative picture – "they're over here in droves, taking our jobs and adding to the waiting times for seeing a GP." It was significant that when the BBC reported the death by starvation of four year old Daniel Pelka in September 2013, no mention was made of his parents' nationality, even though it was obvious from their names, Magdalena Luczak and Mariusz Krezolek, that they were Polish. The Beeb was clearly aware of rising anti-Polish sentiment.

UKIP gained much support in the May 2014 European Parliamentary elections thanks to its tough rhetoric on immigration. The elections took place only four months after the ending of restrictions on workers from Romania and Bulgaria in January 2014. While the number of migrants from these countries employed in Britain actually fell by 4,000 in the first four months of the year, it was still up by 28,000 in the past 12 months. MigrationWatch UK estimated that some 250,000 Romanian and Bulgarian migrants could arrive in the next five years, equivalent to a city the size of Plymouth or Newcastle. Government ministers from these two countries have insisted that these estimates are exaggerated, claiming that most educated Romanians and Bulgarians are likely to choose a southern European country, with which they feel greater affinity. Also, unlike 2004, the whole of the EU lifted restrictions on free movement at the same time on two countries whose combined population is less than that of Poland.

This is not the issue. Quite apart from concerns about Romanian criminal gangs already operating in the UK and allegedly behind 90% of cashpoint crimes, the sentiments of the concerned callers on *Any Answers* is essentially, "When is this deluge ever going to stop?" Unfortunately for them, as long as we remain in the EU, the answer is, "not for a long time." Croatia joined the EU last year and, although its population is currently subject to migration restrictions, these only last until 2018. Meanwhile, further countries are in the queue to join the EU, including Turkey, which has a population twice the size of Poland's. All three of the big UK political parties support Turkish membership, with William Hague, the former Foreign Secretary, particularly enthusiastic. Fortunately, opposition from elsewhere, notably France, means that if ever Turkey joins the EU, hopefully we shall have already left and regained full control over our borders. Historically, UK governments – both Labour and Conservative - have been keen supporters of EU enlargement. The sponsor (or Rapporteur in EU-speak) of Bulgaria's accession was a British MEP, the Conservative Geoffrey van Orden. Theresa May's futile attempt to argue for limits on free movement within the EU shows how this policy has come back to bite her party, although it has not stopped David Cameron endorsing Albania's bid for EU membership.

Why we should be concerned about mass immigration

Immigration is rising up the agenda in other countries too. One factor which helped Tony Abbott win the 2013 General Election in Australia was his pledge to "stop the boats" – in other words, to end the flow of asylum seekers. In a referendum in February 2014, Switzerland voted to curtail its agreement with the EU allowing free movement of people. In France, the *Front National*, led by Marine le Pen, topped the polls in the 2014 European Parliamentary elections after campaigning on an anti-immigration platform. The Netherlands, where similar concerns about immigration have been exacerbated by an economic downturn, was recently described by Mariana Câmpeanu, Romania's Labour Minister, as "xenophobic" and "racist", because 80% of Dutch voters wanted to prevent free movement of people from Romania and Bulgaria.

While there are definitely some unpleasant manifestations of anti-foreigner sentiment, such as the neo-Nazi Golden Dawn movement in Greece, it is grossly simplistic for supporters of free movement of people to view any manifestation of opposition to immigration as a "chilling echo of the 1930s." No one would deny the existence of racism in the EU, or indeed in the UK but, as Ed West points out in his brilliant book *The Diversity Illusion*, there is a big difference between "pathological racism" and "a desire to protect national identity." Large-scale immigration is a legitimate concern not just because of the loss of jobs for UK born workers or longer waits to see one's local GP, but rather because it threatens the cohesion which holds our society together. Since 1945, immigration to relatively wealthy western nations has taken place on an unprecedented scale, thanks to the greater ease of travel. In some parts of UK cities, the native-born white population are in a minority. Between 1998 and 2007, 2 million people moved out of London to live in other parts of the UK. We are in uncharted waters, and we cannot predict how well our country (or others) will cope in the longer term if immigration continues at these levels.

Claims that we always have been a nation of immigrants are not borne out by DNA analysis. Before 1945 the genetic makeup of the inhabitants of the British Isles barely altered in several thousand years, in spite of the invasions of the Romans, Angles, Saxons, Vikings and Normans and the arrival of various immigrants since 1066. The English of 1927 were more than 90% the descendants of the English of 927. This shared genetic inheritance has given us cohesion. It has made us, in Enoch Powell's words, "a single self-conscious entity," a nation composed of what we regarded until recently, in spite of political and social differences as "the same sort of people as ourselves." In the words of the economist Roger Bootle, we "have learned to live together, and often to die together in common cause." Our country has "strong bonds of institutions, common feeling and shared experience." People who feel comfortable with each other are more likely to be willing to share their financial resources and even to make sacrifices for the common good. Following the nuclear reactor disaster at Fukushima in Japan, some workers faced great personal danger by entering the complex to make the damaged reactor safe. Such heroism, widely admired at the time, is far more likely to occur in a society which people regard as being composed as "the same sort of people as ourselves" – in other words, a country with very little immigration. West quotes the socialist academic R. H.

Tawney, who wrote in 1931, "What a community requires.... is a common culture, because without it, it is not a community at all."

The consequences of a nation changing from a community to a society of strangers are spelt out in a study by three academics from Harvard University showing that in the USA, the states with the greatest resistance to the introduction of a European-style welfare state are those which are the most ethnically diverse. In the UK, we are falling out of love with the Welfare State. Kristian Niemietz, a poverty research fellow at the Institute for Economic Affairs observes in his book *Redefining the Poverty Debate*, that "the British Welfare State generates much more resentment and negative attitudes towards its recipients than its counterparts in traditional social democracies " and this is particularly pronounced in areas of high immigration. There is much anger that child benefit payments of £30 million are paid out each year to workers based in the UK but whose families remain in their home countries. Over half of this money goes to Poland and David Cameron has admitted that he is powerless to end this abuse.

Multi-cultural societies are also more violent. The ethnic melting-pot that is Brazil has a murder rate 20 times higher than the UK, and South Africa, the "rainbow nation," has a murder rate 4½ times the global average. By contrast, the lowest crime rates are to be found in countries with little immigration like South Korea and Japan. It is unsurprising, as Ed West also points out, that "throughout history less homogenous societies have tended to require a harsher criminal justice system… None of this bodes well for the future of European liberalism and European welfare systems, which by their very nature, depend on trust". Parts of the UK are already suffering the cost of multiculturalism. Besides the Romanian gangs behind most credit card fraud already mentioned, David Blunkett, the former Home Secretary under the Blair government, has expressed great concerns about the poor relations between Roma migrants and the indigenous population in Sheffield, fearing it could lead to rioting. The Labour Party is belatedly recognising the damage that its open-door immigration policy for Eastern Europeans in 2004 has caused. Jack

Straw, another former Home Secretary in the Blair years, recently called the decision a "disastrous mistake". How sincere is their repentance? Evidence suggests that the creation of "a society of strangers" may have been a deliberate policy on the part of Tony Blair's government. Andrew Neather, a former speechwriter to Tony Blair, claimed that Labour wanted to "rub the Right's nose in diversity." Their driving political purpose, he claimed was "that mass immigration was the way that the Government was going to make the UK truly multicultural."

But multiculturalism has failed, and drastic action is needed to address the mess it has left behind. We cannot go back to the period before 1945 where nationhood and ethnicity were pretty well one and the same thing. However, for the sake of national cohesion, we should do well to heed the comments of the former Israeli Prime Minister Yitzhak Rabin, who once said that Israel must be no less than 80% Jewish. Ed West comments that "few would think {Rabin's comments} an unreasonable expression of national self-determination." Rabin's formula ensures that even allowing for different political opinions among the Jewish majority, they still call the shots as far as the political and cultural direction of the country is concerned. Given that we indigenous Brits have lived here for millennia, it is only right that we too should remain dominant politically and ethnically. To say this isn't "far right" or "racist." The evidence above suggests it is a perfectly logical conclusion to draw for anyone who loves liberty and wants to prevent the state from encroaching further into their day-to-day lives. Government statistics show that in 2011, only 87% of the UK population were UK born,.so there has to be a change of course pretty quickly if we are to avoid dropping below Rabin's 80% threshold.

Furthermore, if moderate and reasoned voices advocating radical change to immigration policy are shouted down by supporters of multiculturalism, the rising anti-immigrant sentiment may find less pleasant outlets of expression. While the BNP, even at its height, never won the level of support enjoyed by Oswald Mosley's "Blackshirts" in the 1930s, we cannot take it for granted that no influential far-right party will ever emerge in this country in the future. Golden Dawn won only 0.23% of the vote in the Greek 2009 elections. In the European Parliamentary elections five years later, it received the third largest share of the vote, gaining three MEPs after polling at 9.4%. You cannot eliminate concerns about loss of national identity by passing equality legislation. It only suppresses the issue. It is frightening to consider that in recent years, there has been a growing trend for armed conflicts to be civil wars rather than conflicts between different countries. Rwanda, Yugoslavia, Iraq, Ukraine, Syria and Sri Lanka all provide a stark warning as to how strongly people can react when they feel that their religion, culture or ethnic identity is threatened from within.

Another way in which immigration erodes our national fabric is through the threat it poses to our countryside. The highest levels of opposition to immigration in a poll for Sky News in October 2013 came from country dwellers. While immigration levels are pretty low in many rural areas (unless there are farms in the vicinity employing large numbers of Eastern European workers), 71% of rural dwellers want drastic cuts in immigrant levels to preserve their tranquillity. Nick Boles, the housing minister, only inflamed tensions when he made a very stupid comment that building houses will create more "human happiness" than preserving green fields. Part of the reason why more houses are needed is because we are living longer, but it is only part of the problem. The arrival of over ½ million immigrants from the EU alone has also had an effect. While most houses built on green field sites and in rural areas will probably not be housing immigrants, a good few may well be inhabited by people moving out of areas which they feel that, thanks to immigration, are no longer inhabited by people like themselves – a phenomenon known as "white flight." The opinion poll proves that Boles is out of step with public opinion. Given a choice between the preservation of our beautiful and varied landscapes or allowing the present levels of immigration to continue, it is a complete no-brainer as to which option the public – rural or otherwise – would choose. We would not need to build so many houses, nor would high house prices cause young people to struggle to get onto the property ladder if immigration were curtailed.

Any solution to the problem will require withdrawal from the EU

A peaceful solution to the growing concerns about immigration will be challenging, and will inevitably be regarded as harsh, but there is no easy alternative. Firstly, Ed West is right to conclude that immigration must be restricted, even if it requires us to withdraw from our international commitments. We must regain complete control of our borders and be able to determine who comes into this country. This requires us to leave the EU and thus extricate ourselves from the principle of free movement of people. Withdrawal from the jurisdiction of the ECJ and ECHR will enable us to return all illegal immigrants and failed asylum seekers to their country of origin. Convicted criminals and beggars from other EU member states must also be sent back to their home countries and not allowed to return. We cannot continue with such absurdities as the recent example of Westminster City Council paying the fares of Roma beggars in London to return to Romania only for them to turn up again a few months later. We need to go further. The taboo of voluntary repatriation must be broken. It is, after all, a win-win situation to help those who do not feel comfortable here to return home. This is hardly "far right extremism", after all, it may just be our weather that they don't like! These people will be happier, while at the same time easing pressure on our housing and infrastructure. We must consider the feasibility of revoking the rights of "permanent residence" currently enjoyed by members from EU member states who have lived here for more than five years. The target of reducing net migration below 100,000 in 2015 is too high. The target should be zero. We really don't need any more immigrants at all, apart from ensuring that we can still attract the best senior professionals and managers in a competitive worldwide market. This sort of traffic is two-way, limited in scale and totally non-threatening. Our national cohesion is not disturbed by a few Japanese bankers working in the City, a Spanish academic teaching at an English university or a Canadian being appointed Governor of the Bank of England. After all, there are UK nationals working in Tokyo's financial sector, teaching in overseas universities or employed as executives of Canadian companies, who are not upsetting the national cohesion of these countries. Free from the EU, we could address any shortages of low-skilled workers by issuing short-term work permits which would not confer long-term residential rights.

A rigid enforcement of tight border controls will also send a message to those thousands of migrants seeking asylum in the UK that the country is closed to them. If you feel you have to flee your country, under United Nations conventions, you should apply for refugee status in the first "safe" country you reach. However, the borderless nature of the EU has allowed this principle to be abused. The closure of the Sangatte detention centre in Northern France in 2002 has not solved the problem, for in December 2013 some 300-500 migrants were camping in the Calais area refusing to seek asylum in France or any other country through which they may have passed. Beggars cannot be choosers and the UK cannot afford to be a soft touch.

After the recent flood of immigrants, we need to stop, pause and allow the UK's current residents - both the indigenous population and those immigrants who love our country and share its historic values - time to work out exactly what being British means in a modern context. Here again, our membership of the EU is a hindrance. The EU has tried to suppress nationalism in a bid to create a common European identity. Instead, its policy of free movement has made many of its citizens more defensive about their national identities - pitting the leaders of member states against one another, as we have seen in the recent heated exchanges over the issue of free movement of people.

Britishness may not be exactly the same as it was 100 years ago, but it must still be rooted in the historic culture and traditions of the indigenous inhabitants, even if some of us have acquired a taste for curry, pasta or reggae! Minorities not happy with the end product of our national deliberations - for instance, those who would rather live under Sharia Law, which has not been and will not be compatible with Britishness – must either accept that their wishes are not acceptable to the majority of the population or else be encouraged to move to a country more in keeping with their preferences.

The USA is a country which has much to teach us here. Until the recent influx of Hispanics, it was remarkably successful in creating a common culture out of people from different ethnic backgrounds. Its founding fathers spoke a common language, believed in limited government and freedom under the rule of law. They shared common interests and attitudes - strongly influenced by the values of Evangelical Christianity, even if many of them were religious sceptics. The USA has had its faults, notably the poor relationship between white and black in the southern states, but the American model created a people proud of its country and culture while their pride helped ensure that immigrants rapidly assimilated, learnt to speak English and adopted many of these same values.

Only when free from the EU can we adopt the positive features of the American model. Free movement between member states has brought a different type of immigrant from the early post-war arrivals, who were predominantly from the Commonwealth countries. They spoke English and came from countries whose legal systems were derived from English Common Law. The Jamaicans, whose arrival on board the *Empire Windrush* in 1948 marked the beginning of large-scale immigration to the UK, had a sense of the UK being their "mother country." The immigrants from Eastern Europe do not feel the same about our land. The EU does not encourage them to feel the same, as it has used multiculturalism as a tool in its futile bid to create a nation called "Europe". It therefore discourages assimilation into the culture of the host nation; statistics bear this out. Far more Indian-born immigrants have applied for UK citizenship and regard themselves as British than their Polish counterparts. Indians may look less like Englishmen than Poles, but they clearly feel a greater affinity with our culture and traditions. When we compare nationality and country of origin, Government statistics show that in the year to September 2011, 696,000 people of Indian birth and 614,000 people of Polish birth were estimated to be resident in the UK, but whereas there were 654,000 Polish nationals, there were only 330,000 Indian nationals. Indians are far more likely to apply for UK citizenship - and therefore to regard themselves as British - than Poles. Given the urgent need to try to rebuild some sort of common national identity, it is absurd that citizens of some our nearest relations, the Anglophone nations such as Australia and the USA, require a visa merely to come to the UK on holiday, but citizens of a country like Bulgaria, with whom we have far less in common, are able to enter the country with no visa, find jobs with very few restrictions and cannot be deported if they commit a crime.

Debunking the claim of economic benefits

Defenders of free movement of people within the EU point to its economic benefits. However, a number of studies have questioned whether mass immigration has actually made us wealthier. Over a decade ago, in a paper entitled *Do we need mass immigration?* Anthony Browne analysed a Home Office report, *The Migrant Population in the UK: Fiscal Effects*, which claimed that immigrants paid £2.5 billion in taxes more than they received in benefits. He pointed out that the report was misleading, as it lumped together the relatively small number of well-paid finance professionals and industrialists with dependent spouses, refugees and immigrants with no qualifications. When the small high-paid minority are excluded, immigrants are a drain on the state. He also pointed out that in the final quarter of the 20th Century, Europe's economic growth was on a par with the USA's in spite of a far lower level of immigration, as was that of Japan, where immigration is minimal.

Of course, more people in a country will almost inevitably result in a higher GDP (the total value of goods and services produced by a country), but the indicator of whether immigration has brought any economic benefit is **GDP per capita** – in other words, per head of population. Statistics from the International Monetary Fund's October 2013 *World Economic Outlook* indicate that the recent arrivals from Eastern Europe have brought very little benefit, as the graph below shows.

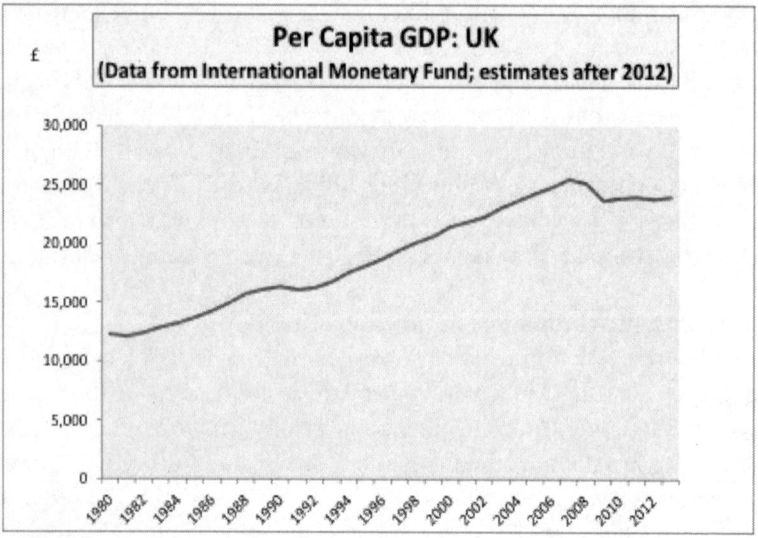

Per Capita GDP adjusted for the effects of inflation ("constant prices" or "real GDP" in economists' jargon) increased by £2,212 in 2000-2004, the four-year period leading up to the accession of the former Soviet bloc states. However, in the nine years from 2004-2013, the latest estimate of the increase is £286, little more than **one eighth** of the growth from 2000-2004, yet over a timespan of nine years as opposed to four. Even though the pro-EU think tank Open Europe supports the principle of free movement of people, in its paper on the subject, it has admitted that "Immigration boosts economic growth but not necessarily prosperity." The IMF statistics also confirm the finding of a report by the House of Lords Economic Committee, published in April 2008, which concluded that "we have found no evidence for the argument, made by the government, business and many others, that net immigration – immigration minus emigration – generates significant economic benefits for the existing UK population". The only conclusion which can be drawn is that **we should have been better off without the influx of Eastern Europeans from 2004 onwards.** Or, to use a future tense, upon withdrawal from the EU, if the vast majority of these people, especially dependent wives and children, were repatriated to their country of origin, it would be a benefit for the indigenous UK population. The negligible increase in overall wealth per head of population since 2004 needs to be weighed against the pressure on schools, hospitals and housing, the loss of jobs for the native community, the number of criminals to have moved to the UK, the cost of translation services and benefit fraud. A Home Office report detailing numerous cases of sham marriages and fraudulent welfare claims involving migrants from the EU has yet to be made public, but the costs are believe to run into millions of pounds. A report by MigrationWatch UK suggests that on average, each immigrant arriving in our country has cost us £3,000.

In the light of these statistics, we need to treat with some scepticism the claim that immigrants are needed to balance the government's books. The office for Budget Responsibility is actually proposing that immigration levels need to be increased and has drawn a graph suggesting that the deficit cannot otherwise be cut. This is highly questionable. The Coalition Government could do far more to bring spending down. There has been no "bonfire of the QUANGOs" as David Cameron promised and expensive vanity projects like the HS2 high speed rail link should be axed. The TaxPayers' Alliance publishes a book called the *Bumper Book of Government Waste* every year, which shows in considerable detail just how spendthrift the government is. The 2013 edition put unnecessary expenditure at £120 billion, or £4,500 per household. This is virtually the same amount by which our national debt is increasing, so it proves that as we emerge from recession and the economy picks up, a more frugal government could balance the books in a few years without relying on immigration.

We are also told that we will need more immigration in the future in order to fund our pensions. It may be true that more young working immigrants provide more money in the state pension pots of those approaching retirement, but it raises the question as to who will pay for these immigrants' pensions when they in turn reach retirement age. Relying on immigration to fund retirement is merely kicking the can down the road. It fails to address the fundamental problem – namely that the UK's welfare state was designed for a period when the fertility rate was higher and people didn't live so long. Whatever one's opinions of their motives, far more people are now choosing to have smaller families or no children at all. The government cannot and should not force people to have more babies, so it needs to look instead at changing the whole structure of pensions in the UK. As Fraser Nelson, the editor of The Spectator, argues, we have to "wean this country off the drug of immigration", which he calls a "counsel of despair". He points out the advantages that would be gained by improving the quality of our educational system, enabling more of our population to undertake skilled work and thus earn more money. This is a valid point. We also need to consider extending our working lives in both directions. Why insist on keeping all children at school until they reach the age of 18? This policy should be reversed, allowing the least academic to leave at 16 or even younger if they are able to find work or an apprenticeship. It would enable these youngsters to contribute to the economy (and their own pension pots) rather than being a drain on the state. Later retirement also would remove any alleged need to increase immigration to fund our pensions. The Welfare State has raised expectations unrealistically. When a modest state pension of five shillings (25p) a week was first introduced in 1908, only the "deserving poor" over the age of 70 were eligible – a tiny percentage of the population at that time. Now we take a larger state pension for granted, and currently receive it at the age of 65 for men and 60 for women. Increasing longevity has made this unrealistic and the government is gradually raising the retirement age, with both men and women being required by 2028 to wait until they are 67 before receiving their state pension. We must alter our retirement expectations regardless of immigration. The prospect of more years in work may not seem very appealing, but actually, working to a greater age should not be viewed negatively by those of us currently under 65. A recent study by Gabriel Heller Sahlgren for the Institute of Economic Affairs has concluded that encouraging older people to stay in work longer provides an important additional benefit to the individual concerned as well as reducing the cost of pension provision. "People seem to be healthier if they continue working rather than spending longer in retirement" he concludes. So extending our working lives by a few years will be good for us, as well as vastly preferable to any short-term attempt to preserve current pension arrangements by unsustainable levels of immigration.

On balance and notwithstanding the many talented individual immigrants who have come to love their adopted country and its culture, statistics show that recent mass immigration has brought far more problems than benefits, politically incorrect as such a conclusion may be. Ed West contrasts the respective behaviour of the UK and Japan in the 1960s when the textile industries in both countries demanded more immigration to do the jobs which, in an age of almost full employment, did not appeal to the indigenous workers. The UK government imported thousands of Pakistanis to work in the textile industry. However, when low-cost imports put our mills out of business, we were left with thousands of unemployed immigrants, sowing the seeds of the Asian ghettos in several towns in the North of England. By contrast, in Japan, the government rejected the demands of business, forcing companies to update their machinery. The Japanese textile industry fared much better in consequence, and the country's ethnic balance was not disturbed.

Of course, were we to leave the EU, it would be foolish immediately to repatriate all the workers from Eastern Europe. The NHS, along with many private businesses, would be unable to find replacement workers at such short notice. However, outside of the EU, we could deal with any skills shortages on more advantageous terms in the short term, while overhauling the country's education system to ensure more of our own population gain suitable qualifications in the longer term. If we repeal EU employment legislation such as the Agency Workers' Directive, we could then invite only such migrant workers as were needed at any given time, allowing them into a country on short-term work permits, with no long-term rights of residence, eligibility for benefits or accrued pension rights and not permitting them to bring their families over, except for holidays. This may sound harsh, but given that migrant workers would still be willing to work here under these conditions, what is wrong with opting for an alternative that is far cheaper than allowing free movement of people? It is like asking why anyone would want to pay £3,000 for an object they could buy for £2,000.

Obviously, some form of negotiation with the EU would be required to determine the terms under which EU citizens could live and work in the UK and vice versa, but any arrangement must of necessity fall short of allowing free movement of people, as no referendum for independence can otherwise be won, Fortunately, even EEA membership would allow us to place restrictions on free movement of people. Liechtenstein, whose relationship with the EU is similar to Norway's, has the right to restrict residency of EU citizens under Articles 112, 113 and Protocol 15 (articles 5-7) of the EEA agreement. Any restriction on migration from the EU may make it harder for UK students to study in European universities or for our pensioners to retire to the Mediterranean sunshine. Restrictions on benefit rights will also cut both ways and UK workers abroad may lose their entitlement to benefits if they lose their jobs, although one has to ask why should UK citizens expect a foreign country to give them money for doing nothing? Until recently, such a scenario would have been unthinkable. However, these are small prices to pay to retain the cohesion of the nation state. Switzerland's decision to impose tight controls on migration from the EU in a referendum in February 2014 was an acknowledgement of this very concern. As the country had signed up to the principle of free movement of people including the EU's Schengen agreement allowing free movement across national frontiers, it was a pretty drastic move, as its whole relationship with the EU will have to be revised. The motives of the voters were clearly not economic, as Switzerland has an unemployment rate of barely 3%, and many of its industries rely on skilled workers from other countries. However, with foreigners accounting for 25% of the Swiss population, the electorate decided that enough was enough. The need to keep Switzerland feeling Swiss outweighed any economic considerations. Given the dubious nature of the claims that immigrants have benefited our economy, it is time that the will of the people in the UK was reflected – by our leaving the EU and regaining control of our borders. The very survival of our country is at stake.

Chapter 10
Withdrawal would be Britain's gift to the world.

One of the most interesting tasks I was asked to do during my time in Brussels was to translate a speech by Jean Rey, a Belgian lawyer who became the second President of the European Commission in 1967. I would not claim to be a fluent French speaker, but I am sufficiently competent to have sensed his warm enthusiasm for the European project – it was almost infectious, dare one say. He saw a great future ahead for the EU and conveyed it with great gusto throughout his speech. Fast forward 47 years and things are very different. The results of the recent European Parliamentary elections prove that, as Ambrose Evans-Pritchard beautifully puts it, "Superstate romantics are on the back foot almost everywhere." However, supporters of a United States of Europe are not going to roll over and admit defeat. David Cameron's battle over the appointment of the arch-federalist Jean-Claude Juncker, the former president of Luxembourg as President of the European Commission proves the point. Juncker's supporters cannot be unaware that he once said of the controversial Lisbon Treaty that, "of course there will be transfers of sovereignty. But would I be intelligent to draw the attention of public opinion to this fact?" The new Commission will doubtless come out with more scare stories about the dangers of rolling back the integration process, but a lot of people are no longer listening. After all, to anyone convinced that going forward means crashing into a brick wall, warnings about the dangers of allegedly going backwards will cut little ice. Open Europe's Director Mats Persson claims that, "if European voters always face the choice between 'more Europe' and 'no Europe', then "sooner or later, they will pick the latter."

Much continental dissatisfaction with the EU revolves around its flagship project, the Euro. The Cypriot-British economist Sir Christopher Pissarides, who was once a supporter of the single currency, told an audience at the London School of Economics in December last year that "the Euro should either be dismantled in an orderly way or the leading members should do the necessary as fast as possible to make it growth and employment-friendly,... Back then {i.e., in 2008, when Cyprus joined the Euro}, the Euro looked like a great idea. But it has now backfired. It is holding back growth and job creation and it is dividing Europe. The present situation is untenable." Like every EU project, the driving force behind the Euro was primarily political rather than economic. It had some serious design flaws, but Europe's politicians overlooked them. Greece was allowed to join the Euro even though it appears that it under-reported how bad its finances were at the time. The net result is that while Germany is thriving with unemployment at just over 5.4% in April 2014, Greece and Spain have endured more than two years of youth unemployment above 50%. One cannot but wonder if it will be possible for all these nations to share a common currency for much longer. Indeed, it is surprising that support for the Euro remains so strong in these Mediterranean countries, as the recent recession would not have hit them so hard if they had kept their own currencies. Given the recent success of anti-austerity political parties in Greece and Spain, claims made by a number of politicians during 2013 that the Eurozone crisis is over are very premature.

Adding to the pressures on the EU is the success of the *Front National* in France. Like UKIP in this country, the party is highly critical of the EU. There, however, the similarity ends. Marine le Pen may not be about to become French president, but her party's success will bolster France's historic protectionism and hinder David Cameron's desire for further trade liberalisation. It is possible that the French may even derail the EU/US Free Trade agreement. Indeed, the EU could find itself torn between keeping either France or the UK in the EU, but not both. If so, we shall be cast off. A French-inspired retreat into protectionism may not go down well with the pro-free market countries of Eastern Europe, but the end of a strong Franco-German axis at the heart of the EU would mean the collapse of the whole project.

All these tensions are likely to bring into question the survival not just of the euro but of the EU itself. Is it, in the words of former Chancellor Nigel Lawson, "past its sell-by date"? Quite probably. It was founded in the early years after World War 2 when large bureaucratic international organisations were in vogue. Unelected "experts" could solve the world's problems, supposedly. Well, they haven't – indeed, they have become part of those problems. Apart from the USA, the most successful economies of the late 20th century were small places like Hong Kong, Switzerland and Singapore where bureaucracy was kept to a minimum.

Withdrawal could be a benefit for the EU

So it makes sense to walk away from this failing project. It would benefit not just the UK but the EU as a whole. It is nonsense for Nick Clegg to tell his Irish counterpart on 13th November 2013 that British withdrawal would, "in many ways impoverish the European Union as a whole." Withdrawal would provide a catalyst to help the remaining member states work out what they want the EU to be. A federal superstate, the United States of Europe, is still the goal of many European politicians and federalist parties won the lion's share of votes in the recent elections. However, the low turnout and the increased support for various protest parties shows that disillusion is on the increase in other countries. Take, for example, the Netherlands, one of the six founder member states. Dutch euroscepticism was virtually non-existent 20 years ago, but the rejection of the European Constitution by Dutch voters in the 2005 referendum was a powerful signal of a change in attitude. This change is gathering pace. The number of voters supporting withdrawal increased from 25% in 2011 to 29% in 2013. Only 13% of the Dutch electorate think that the EU should ultimately become one country. Meanwhile, less than a decade after his country joined the EU, the former Czech president Václav Klaus published his book *Europe – a shattering of illusion*, which called for it to withdraw. The EU has no divine right to eternal life. Indeed, it may be a blessing in disguise if UK withdrawal precipitates some sort of collapse. Only three years after the signing of the Treaty of Rome in 1957, the German economist Wilhelm Röpke had begun to feel uncomfortable about what was evolving. "To try to organise Europe centrally, to subject the Continent to a bureaucracy of economic planning, to weld it into a bloc, would be nothing less than a betrayal of Europe and the European patrimony," he wrote. "The betrayal would be all the more perfidious for being perpetrated in the name of Europe and by an outrageous misuse of that name."

If the UK were to rejoin EFTA, it would re-invigorate this organisation which, after all, we originally helped to bring into existence as a free trade-only alternative to the EU. A bit of competition would do the EU no harm, and indeed, a resurgent EFTA including a successful independent UK may entice other member states to leave. It is possible that the majority of member states may ultimately come to agree with Röpke that the EU has had its day and seek a future for the continent as a free trade area of sovereign states and nothing more. Meanwhile, for the Balkan countries and former Soviet republics currently seeking to join the EU in order to inform the world at large of their new alignment with the Western democratic nations, membership of EFTA would become every bit as effective a statement to this effect, yet without requiring any loss of sovereignty.

On the other hand, it is possible that the EU may recover from all its current woes and we should be the only nation to leave. Still, at least a UK exit would allow the other member states to consider an alternative future, even if they ultimately choose to reject it.

If only the UK leaves and the withdrawal process is undertaken by a Prime Minister who is only obeying the will of the people with extreme reluctance, he need not worry. The history of a nation which reluctantly gained independence from a federation almost 50 years ago offers us great encouragement. Singapore joined the Federation of Malaysia in 1963. Its leaders felt at the time that the historical and economic ties between Singapore and the former British colony of Malaya were too strong for them to continue as separate nations. They had campaigned vigorously for a merger, but having achieved their goal, the union only lasted two years. Following tensions between Singapore and the other Malay states over economic issues and violent clashes between ethnic Malays and ethnic Chinese in Singapore itself, Singapore was expelled from the Malaysian Federation in 1965. Singapore's Prime Minister, Lee Kuan Yew was devastated. "For me, it is a moment of anguish", he said. "All my life, my whole adult life, I have believed in merger and unity of the two territories." However, since 1965 Singapore has never looked back. It has comprehensively out-performed Malaysia, with an economy which has grown by an average of 9% per annum. By 1990, it had become the second wealthiest nation in Asia after Japan.

If tiny Singapore can not only survive as an independent nation but out-perform its larger neighbour, surely the UK, which is one of the world's ten largest economies, is well-equipped to do likewise. Singapore's success also gives the lie to those who say that supporters of UK withdrawal from the EU want to turn the clock back. On 2nd March 2013, Baroness Shirley Williams, interviewed on BBC Radio 4's Today programme in the aftermath of UKIP's strong showing in the Eastleigh by-election, took precisely this line. She suggested that the people who voted UKIP were unhappy about the influence of global financial markets in the modern world. This is nonsense. Globalisation has not caused other nations around the world to share their sovereignty. It has not caused Singapore to have second thoughts and reapply to join the Malaysian Federation. It is benefiting from globalisation as a major financial centre in its own right.

Of course, as this book has shown, our membership of the EU has political as well as economic implications, and supporters of our EU membership claim that withdrawal would cause us to lose influence in the world. This is more nonsense. After all, it is amazing that anyone takes us seriously given our once-proud nation with its great empire can now be bullied into paying fines by an unelected foreign bureaucracy merely for not flying the "Ring of Death" flag. As we saw in Chapter 2, we do not now even have the freedom to determine how to label our bananas!

Who wants to influence what?

If "having influence in the world" means "having influence only as part of the European Union" is this really what we want? Attempts to forge a common EU foreign policy have failed miserably. Whether or not it was right to intervene in Libya, the UK and France waded in, but Germany kept out. The first attempt at a humanitarian intervention under the guise of the EU's Common Security and Defence Force was an unsuccessful muddle. 2,000 EU peacekeepers were sent to the Congo to help supervise free elections in 2005, but did very little to bring peace to the country. As conflict flared up in the east of the country, Javier Solana, the EU foreign policy chief at the time, proposed in late 2008 that a "battle group" of British and German soldiers be deployed to prevent a humanitarian catastrophe. David Miliband, our Foreign Secretary at the time, did something sensible for once. He insisted that action should take place under UN auspices and that the EU should not get involved. This put him at odds with the French Foreign Minister, who supported Solana and EU involvement. Our country has strongly opposed the creation of an EU Foreign Office. Indeed, it was thanks to the UK that Solana's successor, Lady Catherine Ashton, was known as a "High Representative" rather than the "EU Foreign Minister ", even though the difference is only in the title, rather than the function. Our habit of dragging our heels whenever other EU member states have sought to develop the Common Security and Defence Policy illustrates the widespread UK scepticism regarding the claim that in the area of foreign policy, acting together as the EU, the 28 member countries have far greater weight and influence than if they act individually, following 28 different policies. The limited "weight" of the EU was exposed in no uncertain terms by Vladimir Putin in March 2014 when he ordered Russian troops to take control of parts of Ukraine while the EU stood helplessly by. It proves that the idea of 28 nations working together under a common foreign policy just isn't working.

It is best abandoned.

Furthermore, after the débacle of Iraq, two questions must be asked of those concerned about the loss of UK "influence" in the wider world if we leave the EU: what exactly do we wish to "influence" and how do we want to do it? The refusal of our Parliament in 2013 to endorse David Cameron's desire for military intervention in Syria – suggests that Tony Blair's "liberal Interventionism" – interfering in other nations' affairs with the ultimate objective of spreading democracy - is dead in the water. Our capacity to intervene is being eroded anyway by the scaling down of our armed forces. In 1982, at the time of the Falklands War, we were able to deploy two aircraft carriers. We no longer possess a single carrier and there are no plans for us to do so in the coming years. So much for "British influence" in the wider world!

Blair has been the most enthusiastic supporter of our EU membership to occupy No. 10 Downing Street since Edward Heath. He was a particularly vocal advocate of the principle that it offered us greater influence in the world. "When we isolated ourselves in the past", he said in a speech in Birmingham in 2001, "we reduced our sovereignty - leaving us sole masters of a shrinking sphere of influence." It is impossible not to feel a considerable degree of cynicism here. Firstly, one has to ask, at what period in the past was the UK ever isolated? We have been pretty active internationally since the 17th century. Secondly, it is significant that these words were uttered by a man who clearly loves strutting round on the world stage. When the first discussions began about the creation of a post of full-time President of the European Council, Blair was most enthusiastic about the project in the hope that he would be chosen, and gutted when he was passed over in favour of a Belgian nonentity, Herman van Rompuy. Can we also detect from the similar concerns Nick Clegg has expressed about "loss of influence" that he is concerned that UK withdrawal will deny him the chance to pose as a great international superhero?

Returning to the vanguard of democracy

Our country can be far more of an influence for good in bringing freedom to other nations by example than by force. It is quite extraordinary how little interest there has been worldwide in the excellent Swiss political system, which is one of the best, if not the best, in the world. Their system of direct democracy, whereby the voters of the country can hold their politicians to account through binding referendums, ensures that the Swiss government reflects the will of its people better than any other national government. In our country, Common Law established the principle many centuries ago that government rested on the consent of the governed. By the 18th century, we had developed a parliamentary democracy which the French philosopher Montesquieu claimed was the best system to be found in Europe at that time - unique in being constituted for the specific purpose of maximizing political liberty. The best of these principles were adopted later in the century by the newly independent United States of America, and in its turn, the US Constitution became the basis of the Swiss Constitution in 1848. Sadly, in recent years, the Swiss have left us behind. As we saw in Chapter 2, political liberty has decreased in the UK in recent years thanks to our membership of the EU. There are still, nonetheless, some very able thinkers in this country committed to developing a model of accountable, limited government suitable for the 21st century. *The End of politics and the birth of i-Democracy* by the Conservative eurosceptic MP Douglas Carswell argues that the internet age offers us the chance to restore power to the people, while the Harrogate Agenda, the brainchild of another prominent eurosceptic, Dr. Richard North, seeks the same goal, focusing on six objectives which will achieve it – recognition of our sovereignty, real local democracy, separation of powers, the people's consent, no taxation or spending without consent and a constitutional convention.

Given the high profile enjoyed by our country thanks to the Commonwealth and the use of English as the world's language of trade, were we to return to the vanguard of developments in democracy, far more other countries would take an interest than they currently do in Switzerland. However, these exciting possibilities can develop no further until we leave the EU. The claims by Blair, Clegg and others that it would be a "disaster" for us to leave the EU are preposterous. It would be a disaster for us not to leave. We have a long track record of punching above our weight as a nation and can do so again. We need to address various domestic issues first - in particular, scrapping politically correct equality and diversity legislation, ditching nanny-state health and safety rules, sorting out our energy supply and reforming our education system. But we must also address our membership of the EU. It may have made sense 40 years ago when our economy was in such a mess, but it has become an anachronism holding us back from playing a meaningful role in the world of the early 21st century

Conclusion

We are approaching a crossroads as far as our membership of the EU is concerned. There are only two directions to take – in or out. The "in" road appears to have a number of destinations – "reform", "renegotiation", "ever closer union" and possibly "associate membership". However, all of them are, in the Bible's words, part of the same "broad road that leads to destruction." We have seen that however attractively "in" may be packaged, "out" will always be better. Any variety of "in" means that the desire of our best MPs - and many in the population - for our elected parliamentary representatives to have a veto over EU law will continue to be dismissed as "unrealistic." If we care for our country, we cannot allow this absurd situation to continue. In a speech in London on 28th February 2013, Herman van Rompuy, the former President of the European Council, said that leaving the EU was "not a matter of just walking out. It would be legally and politically a most complicated and unpractical [sic] affair...Just think of a divorce after 40 years of marriage. Leaving is an act of free will and perfectly legitimate but it doesn't come for free." This book has not gone into the details of the mechanism of exit, but neither has it ignored the possibility of a few pitfalls en route to re-establishing ourselves as an independent nation. The exit route will be tough. We saw, for instance, in Chapter 7 that there might be a few job losses, although any damage to the UK economy from withdrawal is likely to be far smaller than that caused by giving control of the Treasury to Ed Balls in 2015.

We are currently in a critical situation, like a patient who has just been diagnosed with cancer. Fortunately at this stage, it is not terminal, but Mr van Rompuy is right – a cure will not "come for free." Like cutting out a malignant tumour, independence may be a long and painful process, especially as we have been tied up with the

EU for over 40 years. On the other hand, leaving the tumour of EU membership untreated is far worse and will result in death. "In" under any terms ultimately means the end of the distinctives that make our country what it is, be it through the gradual erosion of our legal system, the increasing impotence of our Parliament, mass immigration or financially ruinous directives. It may be many years before this happens but, unless the EU implodes, that is the only destination on offer at the end of the "in" road. We do not know how many twists and turns our slippery politicians will take before the inevitable referendum takes place, but when it does come, we must seize it with both hands. The spirit that withdrawal would create in our nation will carry us through any short-term problems. It will be like the popular mood when we finally emerged from the Second World War in 1945 and people threw street parties to celebrate their hopes for the future. It will be like the amazing scenes we saw in 1989 when the former Soviet bloc nations threw off the yoke of Marxism. Withdrawal will create an opening to replace the discredited political leaders of today – and perhaps even the parties they lead – by something better, as we saw in Chapter 4. It is an exciting prospect indeed. Like successful cancer surgery, withdrawal from the EU will be nothing less than a new lease of life - a chance for our once-great country to walk tall on the world stage once again.

About the Author

John Petley is somewhat of a latecomer to politics. He read music at Oxford before pursuing a career in IT, interrupted by two years at Moorlands Bible College, where he studied for a diploma in applied theology.

His political involvement began in 2000 when he was handed a leaflet about the European Union. This resulted in him joining UKIP and standing as the party's candidate for the Lewes constituency in the 2005 General Election. He then worked for two years as a researcher in the European Parliament in Brussels.

Although not currently a member of any political party, John is still passionate in his belief that the UK should withdraw from the EU. His research paper *On the Wrong Track*, which highlighted the growing interference of Brussels in the UK railway network, was published by the Bruges Group in 2009. He is Operations manager for the Campaign for an Independent Britain and also edits *Freedom Today*, the quarterly magazine of The Freedom Association, which regularly features articles from several leading proponents of UK withdrawal.

Outside of politics, John enjoys steam trains, classical music, keeping guinea pigs, gardening and country walks. He is married to Katherine and lives in Gloucestershire. An Evangelical Christian, he preaches from time to time in various churches in the south of England.